IS THAT YOU, LORD?

IS THAT YOU, LORD

Practical Methods for Learning Spiritual Discernment

ROBERTA ROGERS

Chosen Books

A Division of Baker Book House Co
Grand Rapids, Michigan 49516

Published by Chosen Books
A division of Baker Book House Company
P.O. Box 6287, Grand Rapids, MI 49516-6287

Printed in the United States of America

Library of Congress Cataloging-in-Publication Data

Rogers, Roberta, 1942–
    Is that you, Lord? : practical methods for learning spiritual discernment / Roberta Rogers.
        p.   cm.
    Includes bibliographical references.
    ISBN 0-8007-9275-0 (pbk.)
    1. Discernment of spirits. 2. Rogers, Roberta 1942-   I. Title.
BV5083.R64 2000
234'.13—dc21   99-059680

For current informaion about all releases from Baker Book House, visit our web site:
http://www.bakerbooks.com

For Bill,
my first editor and God's first "voice" for me,
with love

Father of Light, shine through me
Shine so the whole world will see
All the wondrous things You have done
That they might know that You love everyone
Father of Light, shine through me.

. . . Shine through me
With all Your grace and all Your glory
Let them see just a glimpse of You
Shine through me.

Lisa Adams, *Father of Light*

Contents

Acknowledgments

Like the long lists of begats in the Bible, I used to skip the acknowledgments section in books. Then I realized those names represent real people. Someday I will meet many of them in heaven. Now I read all the names in the Bible and all the notes in books, getting to know some of my brothers and sisters in advance.

As I finish this book, I understand clearly how deep the desire is to thank those who have been part of it. My heart overflows with gratitude for those who have been my help and encouragement.

First and last it is the Lord Jesus I thank. He came to me a quarter of a century ago when I was not really seeking Him. By His Spirit He has loved and nurtured me into the person I am becoming. He has taught me to want to hear His voice, His plans, in every corner of my life. He has enabled me to find tremendous joy in the painful struggle to communicate. He has given me precious and gifted people to help me along.

My husband, Bill, was my first editor. Even though the earliest copy I submitted to him, a news story of a barn fire, contained the elegant if not so newsworthy description *the totality of the conflagration,* he has always believed in my writing gift. He has encouraged me toward excellence. I would not be where I am today without him. Thank you, honey.

The Lord has added a special blessing to Bill's editing in Jane Campbell of Chosen Books. Had I made a list of what I wanted or needed in a book editor, I could not have come up with a better one. She has been honest and deeply encouraging. She has taken time to help me at every turn, going the extra mile of pre-reading and critiquing each chapter. Her comments have been clear and accurate, and the hard ones have been tempered with unmitigated kindness. She is a gifted editor and a most special woman. I am blessed to be working with her.

I send a special thank you to my editors at *Guideposts*, Dick Schneider, Jim McDermott and Andrew Attaway. Over the past few years they, and others there, have nudged and nurtured my fledgling career. Most especially I am deeply grateful for the kind mentoring of John and Tib Sherrill, whom the Lord used to bless my life long before I met them.

I am indebted to the Reverend Dale Becraft for his excellent input and for checking the chapters of this book for theological correctness. I appreciate my pastor, Brent Brooks, for his wise counsel. I thank my special readers, Mary Belote and Angela Dion, for their honest insight. You will meet others (such as Diane Edge), who have contributed stories and ideas, later in this book. I could not have written it without them.

Special thanks to my book club buddies—among them Deb Luehe, Nancy Liggett, Dari McGinnis, Jill Brooks and Rosey Bowman. They have encouraged me month after month and provided prayer-provoking ideas. Susie Best challenged me with superb questions I could not answer. And years ago in Virginia Mary Alcott Beach urged me, "Write, Bobbi! Just write!" long before I did.

Hugs to my four fine sons, now grown to manhood. Tom, John, Peter and David, your "Way to go, Mom!" has been sweet music to my ears. You have enriched not just my writing, but my whole life. I am blessed in knowing each unique one of you. You, too, Sean Bates, Jeanette Vanderlinden, Pete Cofer and all our "extra" children.

Thanks to my cousin Lee Schaffer, who volunteered her editing expertise, and to my mother and brother, who have allowed me to share some personal things that, because of the Lord's love, are no longer painful.

Blessings to Theresa Hudler and Nancy Hutchinson for their never-ending intercession. Very, very special thanks to my weekly prayer partner, Ellen Palmer (and to her husband, Roger, for clipping relevant newspaper items for me!).

Finally, and most importantly, thank *you* for joining me on the journey.

Prologue

Conversations with *What* God?

In the months before I began working on this book, two circumstances prepared me to be ready and willing to write it. The first was receiving a birthday gift—a book from a dear friend just finding her way back to faith. The second was an interview I conducted with a person from a mainline Christian church who had had a near-death experience.

As I started to read the book, and then again as I conducted the interview, my spiritual hair began to stand on end. Both the author and the church member with the near-death experience claimed to have had conversations with God. But by the time I had traveled very far with each of them, I was wondering, *What God?*

In light of these two incidents, my heart longed to help others avoid the discernment mistakes that the book writer, the friend who gave it to me and the person I interviewed had made. I yearned for my friends to have easy, accessible ways to assess things they thought or read. I wanted them to have practical methods to learn spiritual discernment. So when the opportunity came for me to write this book, I was ready and joyously willing.

In the Postscript I will give you the details about that book and the interview. In the meantime let's begin the journey.

o n e

What Is Discernment?

"We have to do something about her. . . ."

One of the women let the words hang.

It was Lent 1974, and Beth Kulow, Dixie Merrill and Janice Ferguson were coordinating an interdenominational Bible study in Newark, Ohio. They had a problem.

"Her intentional arguments against everything we say are confusing the new believers," another agreed. "She dominates and destroys. Scripture says we should ask her to leave the group if she won't change."

"Why don't we fast for a day and then pray together?" the third suggested. "Let's ask God to show us what He wants us to do."

When Beth, Jan and Dixie met to pray, God spoke mutually into each heart: *Let her stay. I am going to do a great thing.*

I was that argumentative, faith-destroying woman. And a week later the Lord did His "great thing." He sovereignly captured me and began a lifelong process of change and renewal in my mind

15

and heart. Although many years passed before I learned what
Dixie, Jan and Beth had done, my new life in Christ had been
prefaced by an act of spiritual discernment: Those women heard
the voice, will and heart of God for a specific situation.

Discernment! The word calls up pictures of supernatural knowing, "seeing within," the ability to comprehend some hidden
truth. For a moment the veil is moved aside and we perceive
the supernatural aspect of a situation. Or we suddenly understand clearly what to say or do.

I see a practical illustration of this in the word processing
program of my computer. When I hit a key that says *Reveal codes,*
my screen full of writing splits into two. The top screen shows
my page as it was. The bottom screen shows the same portion
of manuscript but with the typesetting commands visible. I see
my writing in new detail and can correct errors more easily.

In the same way, the Holy Spirit can enable us to see the spiritual makeup of an idea or problem or situation. We can assess
where the Lord is and where He is not. We can correct our errors
before we "print it out"—that is, act on it. We can discern.

The Greek root of the New Testament word *discern* is *doki-
mazo,* meaning "to test metal." The concept implies approving
something after testing it. The Latin root of *discern* means to
separate by sifting.

When I was a little girl, my parents, brother and I would
escape from our hot city apartment at least one day every summer and drive to my aunt's house near the shore. The highlight
of the day: a visit to a beach on Long Island Sound. There, clad
in a new bathing suit, I was given a small shovel and a sifter. I
scooped sand into the gaily painted metal hoop, then shook it
back and forth. Slowly the sand filtered through the wire mesh
until only tiny, translucent, periwinkle shells were left—"gold"
to a city child.

At Sutter's Mill in California, men panned for real gold. And
for ages before that, housewives similarly shook their wheat,
letting the chaff float away on the wind. This is sifting—separating the valuable from the worthless.

Likewise spiritual discernment is letting the Holy Spirit help us sift the true from the false, the helpful from the useless, sometimes even the best from the better. In the chapters ahead, we will see there is a cry in our heavenly Father's heart for *all* His children to grasp this ability to discern. He wants every one of us to learn to sift ideas, thoughts, emotions and situations that come into our lives every day. He wants us to "pan" through the mud of this world's ideas—and our own and our enemy's—to find the purest gold of His will and His love.

Why Do We Need to Discern?

As believers we rely on spiritual discernment for many different needs. We can, for instance, be given a special anointing in order to "test the spirits" (1 John 4:1) while waging spiritual warfare. As with all discernment, this is an awesome gift—and a great responsibility. Knowing the source of information means that those doing the warfare can pray in such a way that any evil principalities and powers dominating the situation in the unseen side of life (see Ephesians 6:12) are defeated at God's command.

Or we might need specific direction, as did Dixie, Jan and Beth, and want to be certain that the plan we receive is from God.

But probably our most prevalent need for discernment relates to the innumerable thoughts and ideas we have throughout each day. A thought or plan pops into your mind. Is it the Lord speaking? Your own desire? The enemy? This is the area we will be addressing in this book.

Spiritual discernment is critical for every believer. Before we believed, we walked, as the Bible puts it, "in the world" (Ephesians 2:12). Now we live in a different Kingdom with a very different value system. (We will discuss this in chapter 3.) We must learn a new way of thinking about everything. If we are to walk in the will of the Lord, learning to follow His direction one day and one event at a time, we must be able to distinguish His voice from all others. Sound like a formidable task? As you will see, you can indeed learn to answer with assurance a key question: "Is this You, Lord?"

As we begin to sift truth from falsehood, the Lord promises, "If you bring out the precious from the worthless, you shall be My mouth" (Jeremiah 15:19, MLB). We *will* hear His voice and, in turn, become His voice to others.

Walking in Discernment

When I speak of discerning God's "voice," I include His will, His plans, His promises, His love—anything God wants to communicate to and through you and me. It encompasses what He wants and how and when He wants it.

I do not intend this book as a theological treatise on discernment. In the pages ahead I write from the context of my own life, enhanced by what I have heard or read from others. Throughout I will share what I have learned, even as I look ahead to where I know I have yet to go.

My journey is not yours. You are the only *you* ever created; your life and spiritual journey are unique. Just as I have learned to turn personally to the Lord for specific answers to specific questions in my own life, I hope you are doing the same, and that this book will help you do so even more. I pray that the Holy Spirit will lead you into all truth, one day at a time, in the context of your special life.

Sifting your thoughts and emotions can become a most practical process. God promises that He will help you—and that you will discern His help. Jesus said, "You will know the truth, and the truth will set you free" (John 8:32).

As we will see in the chapters ahead, the process of seeking the truth turns us to the Lord over and over.

- It teaches us to pray, to listen, to know His voice and to hear His heart above the clamor of the world, the enemy and our own desires.
- It gives us practice in obeying Him.
- It teaches us how to learn from failure and move forward.
- It makes God part of our everyday lives here on earth.
- Most important it makes us more like Jesus, who always listened to and heard from His Father.

In the next chapter we will begin our journey with the premises and promises God has given us about seeking and finding that truth that will set us free.

Once Over Lightly

Although learning spiritual discernment may sound intimidating, the process of sifting our thoughts and emotions down to their very sources, and seeking the Lord's voice to us in them, can become a very practical process. Our Heavenly Father's heart cries out for us to learn to hear and follow His voice. Step by step His Spirit will help us on this lifelong, life-changing journey.

Your Turn to Discern

1. As you travel this journey with me, turn to the Lord at each step and ask Him, "Is this idea something You want to add to my life right now? Or is it for later? How do You want me to apply it? Have You already begun or

done this in my life?" Here is a prayer to get you started: "Lord, You know all the right ways to help me grow up in You. You know the right time to teach me new things, such as deeper discernment. Help me learn to hear Your voice more clearly."

2. Because the Lord's voice can never violate Scripture or a scriptural principle, why don't you make it a habit to look up all the Scripture references in these chapters, starting with this one, and discern for yourself what I share?

two

Premises and Promises

Does our incredible Creator God, King of the universe, really want to communicate with us personally? What does the Bible say about His willingness to speak to us and about His help as we learn to hear Him?

Let's see what Scripture says about spiritual discernment, and find some special promises regarding discernment that the Lord has made to us.

Discernment: Thinking about Thinking

"Boy, I shouldn't have said . . . !"

"Oh, dear, I wish I hadn't. . . ."

"How could I ever have thought . . . ?"

Twenty-twenty hindsight is perfect. How clearly you can evaluate what you did, once it has been said or done! Wouldn't it be wonderful to have a way to check out an idea before you act? Well, God had just that in mind when He created you. He enabled you to think about what you are thinking.

You can think a thought: *That woman's dress is too fussy.*

Then you can think about that thought: *That wasn't very charitable of me. Why am I always so judgmental? Besides, the dress isn't fussy, really. It just isn't her style.*

You can even think about what you did about that thought: *I'm so glad I didn't say anything about her. She's that woman who lost a lot of her clothes in a fire last week. Boy, would I have been embarrassed!*

God gave us this unique ability to think and then to analyze what we just thought. We can choose to act or not act based on what we think about any given thought or idea or plan.

From Scripture we learn that God has a purpose in blessing us with this incredible ability: He wants us to learn to sift out—to discern—and then to follow the truest and best ideas, thoughts and plans.

His ideas, thoughts and plans.

His ideas, thoughts and plans just for *us.*

Just for *you.*

Before I knew the Lord, it never dawned on me that I ought to check the sources of thoughts that bombarded me hundreds of times a day. I filtered them subconsciously through my current needs and feelings, my lifestyle and my hodgepodge philosophy. Then I decided, on some nebulous basis, whether or not to take action on those ideas. Usually, if I liked an idea, I acted. If I did not like an idea, I refused to act on it, or I did it and then pouted. Self reigned.

By the time the Lord broke in on my life, I had spent 31 years constructing my own way of responding to life, to others, to myself. I was an angry woman, frustrated in my marriage, rebelling at the repetitive routines involved in raising three (later, four) little boys. I was an agnostic and dancing around the fringes of the feminist movement. The "women's liberation" ideas fed my anger and dissatisfaction. Getting out and doing my own thing sounded good to me.

22

Mostly I was angry and disappointed with myself for failing to find contentment in the roles of wife and mother. I sensed there had to be another way to respond to the daily circumstances I so disliked, but for the life of me I could not find it. For several years I searched restlessly for what I called "the five o'clock God." I wanted a God who could give me energy and patience at five every afternoon when those three little boys wanted "Up!" "Down!" "Cookie!" "Joooce!" "Mommee!"—and all *I* wanted was to lie down somewhere quiet and breathe. I needed a God of grace and power who loved mothers and small children.

I had very specific ideas, however, about what I would and would not believe about this God, when and if I ever found Him. As a teenager I had "accepted Christ" at a Youth for Christ meeting. By the time I reached college, I had renounced that episode in my life. In fact, it embarrassed me to think about it. I knew I would never again accept the idea that Jesus could be the *only* way to God, and I would never believe the Bible was God's Word. I scoffed at the idea of a God who might be so narrow-minded as to have only *one* true way and *one* true Book.

This gives you an inkling of what the Holy Spirit was up against one day in April 1974 when He opened the door of my life and walked in. I had flopped down for a hard-won nap that rainy Monday afternoon. To calm myself from the hassle of getting one son off to kindergarten and two more down for a nap, I read a few pages in a book on praising God that someone had encouraged me to take a look at. Sleepily I asked something like, "Lord, if You're there, I'd like to learn to praise You this way." I assumed He understood that I wanted "No Jesus, no Bible!" Then I turned over to take my nap.

I never got there. To my amazement, joy and unending thanks, the presence of God took that tiny opening and inundated my life. His love and power seemed to be all around and inside me. From that moment I knew I would never be or think the same, about God or Jesus or the Bible—or anything.

At a meeting that evening I dashed up to Beth, one of the Lenten Bible study leaders who had prayed for discernment about me less than a week before. Excitedly I poured out what had happened. The disbelief on her face must have resembled that of the astonished believers who met the new Paul fresh from his trip to Damascus (see Acts 9:3–19).

Years later Janice, another of the three leaders, wrote me, "Beth called me later that night in absolute shock. *Never* had we seen an answer to prayer work so dramatically . . . and drastically!"

Like every believer, I had entered a whole new world called the Kingdom of God. Here, I would find, the ground rules and priorities are totally different from those of the world in which I had grown up. A renewing process had begun, the goal of which is that every part of my life will ultimately be conformed to the image of Jesus Christ. (We will cover this in more detail in the next chapter.)

Discernment: New Thinking about Old Ideas

For me the first bastion to fall before the light of God's truth had to be my mind. I needed to learn to think about what I was thinking. I had to think about old ideas in new ways.

My old attitude about the Bible was changed in a hurry. At that time I was proud of my role as devil's advocate at the Lenten Bible study. I enjoyed deliberately refuting every Scripture being taught. Quickly the Lord turned that pride back on me. The reasoning went something like this: I now knew that God was real and that He was *much* bigger than I could ever imagine. I had to acknowledge that anything man could do that was in any way good or true, a perfect God could do a million times better.

At that time my husband, Bill, who is a man of high integrity, was a newspaper editor. I knew he sent his reporters out again and again to check the accuracy of major stories before they went to print. He read and edited the most important articles himself. Things he wanted in got in; things he wanted out died before they hit the press. Readers could trust him to do his level best to be truthful and unbiased.

If my imperfect human husband could do these things reliably, it took no stretch of my imagination to know that a Being worth the name of God could do them all perfectly. Thus God could see to it that a book was written and edited to His full satisfaction. He could ensure that every word and concept in it was His. What He wanted in would get in; what He wanted out would get lost. By His Spirit He could move through the hearts of fallible men to write and edit perfectly for Him. No mistakes.

Suddenly I knew I was wrong in my long-held belief that the Bible could not be totally and singularly God's words. I found, to my delighted chagrin, that I could believe Scripture was indeed God's truth. The basic tool for hearing the Lord's voice was now *my* tool.

The bedrock of Scripture is the foundation on which this book you are reading rests. The Bible contains the ultimate truth about the Truth.

How do *you* see this unique Book?

Discernment: A Race and Its Goals

Early in my new faith, I discovered "goal Scriptures" tucked away here and there in the Bible. These are passages that point to specific attitudes and behaviors (goals) toward which the Lord will take me over the years of my growth in Him. The goal Scripture for prayer, for example, is "pray continually" (1 Thessalonians 5:17); for praising God it is "be joyful always" (1 Thessalonians 5:16). These are clear directives. But I find that whenever I come upon goals like these, I groan, "God, I can't do that!"

The peace of the Holy Spirit, however, settles quickly into my heart. I do not have to achieve it all this minute, nor do I have to do it on my own. In the Kingdom of God, I have learned, running the race is as important as attaining the goal. Beginning is the start of winning—and the Lord is with me all the way.

Let's talk about races for a moment. Several times in his letters Paul likens our Christian growth and calling to a race (see Acts 20:24; 1 Corinthians 9:24; Galatians 2:2; 5:7; 2 Timothy 4:7.) The concept is best laid out in Hebrews 12:1–2:

> Since we are surrounded by such a great cloud of witnesses, let us throw off everything that hinders and the sin that so easily entangles, and let us run with perseverance the race marked out for us. Let us fix our eyes on Jesus, the author and perfecter of our faith.

JACKI'S RACE

A dear acquaintance of mine, Jacki Burkhardt, is a home-schooling mother of five, caretaker for her mother-in-law and a niece, and mentor to anyone who needs her. Last fall she sailed up to me after church one Sunday, her eyes aglow.

"Bobbi, guess what? I ran the Marine Corps Marathon! And I finished!"

I gaped down at her petite form. "Jacki! How did you do it?"

"Well, I started walking-running-walking about a year ago. When I got to running two miles straight, I told Eric I was going to aim for the marathon. He thought I should start with a shorter race, but I needed something impossible. It was that goal that made me continue to run."

I listened, fascinated, as around us adults chatted over coffee and doughnuts, and children just let out of Sunday School scampered about the lobby.

"For the first four hours of the race I ran and jogged pretty much O.K. But at twenty miles I hit the wall. I could hardly lift my feet. It got worse and worse. At mile twenty-five I could hardly see. My tongue and fingers were swollen; I had no sweat left. I couldn't stand upright. The last hill lay just ahead. Then suddenly Eric ran down the hill toward me with water and a banana and encouragement. I drank the water and ate the banana. He ran alongside me until I had enough strength to get to the top of the hill, and then it was flat to the finish. There was my family, yelling and cheering! It took me six hours and twenty minutes, two-and-a-half to do the last five miles, and I was one of the very last ones allowed to complete the race. But I did it. I made it!"

Jacki had run with perseverance the race set before her. And she had reached her goal.

OUR RACE

In this world, if you do not finish first, you are soon forgotten. But the racing rules in the Kingdom of God are different. I am running my very own laps in a lifelong marathon. I run on my own track with my own personal trainer. I am not racing against other people but against the old ways I used to be or to respond or to think. Sometimes I might be running a heat against "the powers of this dark world" (Ephesians 6:12). I am running both with and toward the Lord, toward a life fully renewed by Him.

Just as Jacki's family cheered her on to the tape, my grandstands are filled with the cheers of those who have won their races, who have kept the faith and who know that by God's grace, I will, too. Jesus is my Coach, and on Him I keep my eyes as I aim for a finish line overhung with goal Scriptures: "Be patient" (James 5:7); "In your anger do not sin" (Ephesians 4:26); "Forgive [your brother]" (Luke 17:3); "Love your enemies" and do good to them (Matthew 5:43–48).

When I stumble over a hurdle—that is, sin (or, as the Greek puts it, miss the mark)—I can receive forgiveness and press

27

on, "forgetting what is behind and straining toward what is ahead" (Philippians 3:13).

Eric came with food for Jacki and ran along beside her. My Coach is actually, by His Holy Spirit, *in* me to give me renewed strength, courage and vision. His very own power empowers me. Psalm 94:18 says: "When I said, 'My foot is slipping,' your love, O LORD, supported me." And Psalm 18:36 promises: "You broaden the path beneath me, so that my ankles do not turn."

If the hurdles get higher, my Trainer has promised me faith like the feet of a deer (see 2 Samuel 22:33–34; Psalm 18:33; Habakkuk 3:19) to enable me to clear them (see Psalm 18:29). If you have ever seen a frightened stag leap clear over a two-lane highway, as I have, then you know what deer's feet can do.

Ultimately, as Isaiah 40:31 says, I will be given the wings of an eagle and soar over the hurdles. I can hardly wait!

OUR GOAL IN DISCERNMENT

As I share what sounds like an impossible goal Scripture for this heat of our life races, the one called "discernment," do not let its magnitude discourage you. Hang the goal in front of you and set out with confidence. With God, winning is not just *being* there but *getting* there. It is the practice, the falling and getting up, the pressing on to where the blessings lie. Perseverance—staying in the race to the end—is the goal. You begin to win with the first step. As Jacki found, it gets easier as you practice.

With this in mind, my goal Scripture for discernment is 2 Corinthians 10:5: *"We take captive every thought to make it obedient to Christ"* (emphasis added). Ultimately *every* thought we have will be taken to Jesus. We will learn to evaluate everything through one filter: What does the Lord say about this?

Fortunately God has given us both premises and promises about discernment to encourage us in our race.

Scriptural Premises about Discernment

A premise (from the Latin "to send before") is a proposition (idea) on which an argument is based and from which conclusions are drawn. Before we launch into practical aspects of learning to discern, there are premises, or ground rules, that the Lord has given us in the Bible. Six of those premises are:

1. The Bible is our final arbiter of truth.
2. God discerns everything correctly.
3. We do not discern everything correctly.
4. God wants us to discern correctly.
5. As part of the previous premise, God wants us to test everything.
6. We must commit to acting on our learning.

PREMISE 1: THE BIBLE IS OUR FINAL ARBITER OF TRUTH

Because the Bible is God's Word, it can make its own claims about itself. Our choice is to believe these claims or not. Peter wrote in a letter to the new churches:

> Above all, you must understand that no prophecy of Scripture came about by the prophet's own interpretation. For prophecy never had its origin in the will of man, but men spoke from God as they were carried along by the Holy Spirit.
>
> 2 Peter 1:20–22

Earlier in the same chapter Peter stated:

> His divine power has given us everything we need for life and godliness through our knowledge of him who called us by his own glory and goodness. Through these he has given us his very great and precious promises, so that through them you may participate in the divine nature and escape the corruption in the world caused by evil desires. . . . And we have the word of the prophets made more certain, and you will do

well to pay attention to it, as to a light shining in a dark place, until the day dawns and the morning star rises in your hearts.

verses 3–4, 19

As I shared earlier, after the Lord broke in on my life, my mind and heart were changed very quickly where Scripture was concerned. The "morning star" had begun to rise in my heart. It became easy to choose to believe that the Bible was God's own Word. I hope it is for you, too.

PREMISE 2: GOD DISCERNS EVERYTHING CORRECTLY

Theologians call this omniscience—God's supernatural ability to know everything. "Nothing in all creation is hidden from God's sight" (Hebrews 4:13). "The Lord searches every heart and understands every motive behind the thoughts" (1 Chronicles 28:9).

How we deny this! We humans assume we can think anything we want because our thoughts are private. But God knows them, every one of them.

He reminds us in Isaiah 55:9, moreover, that "as the heavens are higher than the earth, so are my ways higher than your ways and my thoughts than your thoughts." We will talk about this in chapter 3, "The Renewed Mind." Things are totally different in the Kingdom of God. It is *our* thinking that has to change, not His.

PREMISE 3: WE DO NOT DISCERN EVERYTHING CORRECTLY

Often we humans are unable to discern the truth at all. "'My thoughts are not your thoughts, neither are your ways my ways,' declares the Lord" (Isaiah 55:8). "The heart is deceitful above all things and beyond cure. Who can understand it?" (Jeremiah 17:9).

In Hebrew tradition *heart* refers to our whole intellectual and emotional makeup, more like what we mean by heart, mind and soul. Jesus substantiated this concept when He said, "Out of the heart come evil thoughts, murder, adultery, sexual immorality, theft, false testimony, slander" (Matthew 15:19).

Yet we live in a world that believes that man and his brain are like God. Man is thought to be basically good, wise and discerning. We think we can use our intellects to solve all our problems.

These were the philosophical tenets of my liberal arts college, and I agreed with them unthinkingly. The idea that man cannot really discern clearly or think like God startled me. If you find it difficult to believe that our incredible human minds are really so muddled that we cannot produce fully accurate concepts or ideas, why not stop and ask the Lord about this? Think of some examples in which man has had great knowledge—and no wisdom. (Splitting an atom and not knowing what to do with the energy or the waste products is one. Inventing a complex computer and forgetting to tell it how to adjust its clock to a new century is another.)

Remember, Jesus promised us that the Holy Spirit, "whom the Father will send in my name, will teach you all things and will remind you of everything I have said to you" (John 14:26). The Holy Spirit will help you learn to discern.

PREMISE 4: GOD WANTS US TO DISCERN CORRECTLY

In Deuteronomy 30, an Old Testament chapter about choices, Moses speaks for God, offering the Israelites the chance to choose between obedience and disobedience. In the last verse he sums up why this is important: "That you may love the Lord your God, listen to his voice, and hold fast to him." God has a voice; He wants us to choose to hear it.

In the New Testament we are commanded to go even further: "Do not conform any longer to the pattern of this world, but be transformed by the renewing of your mind" (Romans 12:2).

In choosing to believe Jesus Christ, you and I have been reborn as God's children—and as His heirs. We are destined

31

to be conformed to the image of His firstborn, Jesus. We are to be made over, made new, made real in this life for a life that lasts for all eternity: "For those God foreknew he also predestined to be conformed to the likeness of his Son, that he might be the firstborn among many brothers" (Romans 8:29).

Jesus had perfect discernment. God wants us to work toward becoming like Him.

PREMISE 5: GOD WANTS US TO TEST EVERYTHING

The dictionary defines *test* as "a means of examination, trial or proof; a criterion or standard." A test can help us examine something to prove its truth. A test can also be administered to help us see our strengths and weaknesses so we can improve.

God Himself will test us. The Bible promises us trials all through our lives "because you know that the testing of your faith develops perseverance" (James 1:3). Our tried and tested faith is very precious to God. This proving, however, is two-way. God asks us to "prove" Him, too, to put Him to the test.

"Wait!" you say. "Doesn't Scripture say, 'Do not put the Lord your God to the test'?"

Absolutely! Jesus quoted Deuteronomy 6:16 when He wrestled with Satan in the desert (see Matthew 4:7). One of the things He meant was that we do not get to set up the parameters of a test or experiment. With very few exceptions (we will talk about Gideon's fleece in chapter 5), we cannot arbitrarily ask God to do something supernatural just so we or someone else can believe. Yet we find throughout the Bible that once we do believe, God asks us to test—to check out or try out—His promises to us.

It is like the process I used to buy my very first new car last summer. I went to several car dealers, picked up their brochures and read them, poked around the outsides of some vehicles and asked a few questions. Then, based on my faith that particular ones would respond as advertised, I climbed in and took them for a test drive. Some of the cars lived up to their promises; some did not. But our God always lives up to His nature and promises, and He wants us to "road test" them in our own lives.

We start with the most basic statement about Himself that God makes: *I am*. From this first step of faith, believing that He *is*, we are told to test, or check out:

1. Ourselves
2. Our actions
3. God's own will
4. The spirits
5. Everything

1. WE TEST OURSELVES

"Examine yourselves to see whether you are in the faith; test yourselves. Do you not realize that Christ Jesus is in you—unless, of course, you fail the test?" (2 Corinthians 13:5). The first test is to make sure Christ Jesus is in you. You must be sure you have specifically asked Him to be there and are not just assuming that over the years of your spiritual journey, He has somehow arrived.

That moment of choice may explode with fireworks and great emotion, or it may occur as a natural "Why, of course, Lord, come right in!" Regardless of how it comes, there has to be a time when each of us deliberately asks for the Lord to take over our lives. There must be a conscious surrender of all we are to Him. We may have to reaffirm that surrender to ourselves at various stages of our pilgrimage, but in His sight, once made, the decision is irrevocable. I may have renounced Him after my tenuous teenage conversion, but He never renounced me. How eternally grateful I am!

2. WE TEST OUR OWN ACTIONS

"Each one should test his own actions. Then he can take pride in himself, without comparing himself to somebody else" (Galatians 6:4).

33

Our actions and behaviors, as we will see in the chapter ahead, flow out of our attitudes and beliefs. So not only are we to take captive or test our thoughts, as 2 Corinthians 10:5 directed, but we are to measure our behaviors against God's standard as well.

Wonderfully, there will come moments along the way when we see our growth and know we have been permanently changed. We need no one else to compete against or to compare ourselves with. We are pleased with our progress in our private races. We feel humbled that God could do this to or through us. The ultimate joy comes when we see Jesus' outstretched arms and hear His magnificent words, "Well done, good and faithful servant!" (Matthew 25:21).

Here is a personal example. I am a talkative, outgoing person. I keep little to myself, good or bad. My poor husband, Bill, often suffers from "M.E.G.O." (My Eyes Glaze Over) when I launch into an emotional subject. So you can imagine how stunned I was when, immediately after discovering the most wonderful secret in the universe, God's love in Jesus Christ, I knew absolutely that I was *not* to talk about it with still-agnostic Bill.

Within days of my April conversion, I read 1 Peter 3:1–4 where women are shown the blessings of "a gentle and quiet spirit." This was certainly something I had never possessed, but I knew the premise was right: I needed to keep mostly silent and let my new lifestyle show Bill its validity.

About two months later we had friends in for dinner one evening. At the table the male guest somehow launched into a discussion of religion. I had sat silent, praying inside, while he talked.

"I see religion as a crutch for weak people," he concluded. Then he turned to me. "Well, Bobbi, I can tell just by looking at you that you don't agree with me. What are your thoughts?"

What could be more tremendous for a new believer than to have someone ask about her faith? My heart beat quickly.

I opened my mouth to begin . . . and not a word came out. I was speechless.

There was a silence. Then, from the other end of the table, came Bill's soft, strong voice. "I tend to agree with you, Frank. I think religion can be a crutch. But she has found something different."

I did not need to say a word. In spite of the fact that his own faith would not bloom for almost a year, Bill was actually testifying about the changes God had made in me. Instantly, beyond my astonished joy, I sensed a warm *Attagirl!* glow all through me. I had let God keep me silent. I had begun to have a gentle and quiet spirit. *I was being changed.*

3. We Test God's Own Will

"Be transformed by the renewing of your mind. Then you will be able to test and approve what God's will is—his good, pleasing and perfect will" (Romans 12:2).

This is our goal in renewing our minds: to be able to test God's will. He wants us, with our muddled minds, to begin to road-test His nature, His words, His ways, His promises and truths. He wants us to discern His good, pleasing, perfect will for us, individually, in the context of the lives you and I are living this very moment.

4. We Test the Spirits

"Dear friends, do not believe every spirit, but test the spirits to see whether they are from God, because many false prophets have gone out into the world" (1 John 4:1).

What are these spirits we are to test? And how do we do it? Again, we will address this in ensuing chapters. Sometimes it is the demonic that we are seeking to unmask. Sometimes it is the world's "spirit," a philosophy created by man, that we need to discern. Sometimes it is a concept we have been taught to believe. We need to sift down to the source of what we are hearing or feeling or reading or seeing. In chapters 5 and 6 I will share some of the ways I—and others—have learned to do just that.

5. WE TEST EVERYTHING

"Test everything. Hold on to the good" (1 Thessalonians 5:21). This statement comes at the end of a passage that warns about the end times. While it refers specifically to the two verses preceding it—"Do not put out the Spirit's fire; do not treat prophecies with contempt"—it is still an excellent approach toward every idea we hear, prophetic or not. It is part of taking every thought captive to Christ.

It might sound as if discernment could soon become a burdensome, 24-hour-a-day project. This is not God's intent at all. His goal is to make us more and more aware of His presence and His love every day until we are home with Him. Turning to Him a dozen or a thousand times a day never burdens Him. If it becomes a burden instead of a blessing for us, we need to stop and assess our motivation in learning to discern. We can ask the Lord to make discernment a joy again. See the section entitled "Going Too Far" at the end of this chapter.

PREMISE 6: WE MUST COMMIT TO ACT ON OUR LEARNING

"Do not merely listen to the word, and so deceive yourselves. Do what it says" (James 1:22). Underlying all the premises of hearing God's voice, of knowing His will, lies one iron-clad commitment on our part: We must willingly choose to obey what we hear. Hearing from God is nothing more than an intellectual pursuit if we have not set the sails of our will to follow the wind of His Spirit.

Yet here we have an incredible, dual-faceted promise: "It is God who works in you to will and to act according to his good purpose" (Philippians 2:13). Not only does God direct us into paths of obedience through His Holy Spirit, but after we discern His will, He also gives us the desire to follow His leading. In the example I shared earlier, God helped me to *want* a gentle and quiet spirit; then, at the dinner party, He showed me He was giving me one.

In our very human weakness, God Himself enters our being to enable us to will and then to act in accordance with His "good purpose."

Scriptural Promises about Discernment

Along with premises about discernment, God has given us promises. A few of these are:

1. We have the mind of Christ.
2. We will know His voice.
3. Discernment is an obtainable, lifelong process.
4. Our training to discern the best enables God to perfect us.

PROMISE 1: WE HAVE THE MIND OF CHRIST

"'For who has known the mind of the Lord that he may instruct him?' But we have the mind of Christ" (1 Corinthians 2:16).

What an incredible resource! Once we are utterly His, by the indwelling Holy Spirit, we have access to the very mind of God Himself. His mind is inextricably intertwined with His unfathomable love and power toward us, and through us to others. Under His wing the possibilities are endless.

On a day-to-day basis, "having the mind of Christ" refers to our knowing and agreeing with what the Bible has to say on any topic. But sometimes having Christ's mind on a matter can be very personal.

Although it had long been the deepest dream of my heart, the door to being a published writer did not open for me until I was 51 years old. Then, after several years of happily writing magazine articles and devotionals, I began to think about writing a book. I longed to share some of the wonderful things I had learned on my pilgrimage. I asked God if this were His desire growing in my heart.

"If it isn't, Lord," I prayed, "just take it away."

The desire grew stronger. I dug out notes from studies and seminars I had presented and made a list of possible book topics. Nothing seemed to jump out at me. But in quiet moments, when I thought about the idea of a book, the jittery excitement remained. It became almost an irritant. Finally, a few months later on vacation, scuffing along the sand on Topsail Island, North Carolina, I prayed, "Lord, the desire to write a book is still there. If it's Your idea and You have something I can share for and with You, I would love it. But I don't have a clear topic in my mind. I'd like one before this vacation ends, or else I'd like You to take this intense desire away."

The days passed quickly. On the day before Bill and I had to pack up, I took the usual walk up the beach.

"Lord, I am on my last quiet walk. I still have no specific idea for a book. If I have none before I reach the cottage, I will understand that this desire is not Yours for me at this time."

I turned back south at the old Topsail tower. Suddenly, between steps, one word dropped clearly into my head.

Discernment.

"Thank You, Lord!" I whispered, my heart thumping.

I had the mind of Christ on the matter.

PROMISE 2: WE WILL KNOW HIS VOICE

"When he has brought out all his own, he goes on ahead of them, and his sheep follow him because they know his voice. But they will never follow a stranger; in fact, they will run away from him because they do not recognize a stranger's voice. . . . My sheep listen to my voice; I know them, and they follow me."

John 10:4–5, 27

These are wonderfully comforting statements! Our Lord knows that we really are like dumb sheep. We apprehend spiritual things slowly, as if our brains are full of wool. We are not to worry, however, because Jesus, by His Holy Spirit, will enable us to know His voice and to listen and obey once we hear it. His voice is more than His words; it is His very way of thinking and acting and reacting, slowly replacing our old, natural way of responding.

PROMISE 3: DISCERNMENT IS AN OBTAINABLE, LIFELONG PROCESS

"Solid food is for the mature, who by constant use have trained themselves to distinguish good from evil" (Hebrews 5:14).

Take heart! As you practice the process of taking every thought captive to obey Christ, you will become more consistent, or mature. Others who have run their races before us learned to discern good from evil, and we will, too. (In the last chapter we will hear from some of those others.)

PROMISE 4: OUR TRAINING TO DISCERN THE BEST ENABLES GOD TO PERFECT US

"[May] your love . . . abound more and more in knowledge and depth of insight, so that you may be able to discern what is best and may be pure and blameless until the day of Christ" (Philippians 1:9–10).

Practice will make you "perfect." You will be able to discern not only what is good, but what is best, and this wisdom will help keep you "pure and blameless" until the Lord comes. What a precious promise and a secure hope!

A Warning and a Comfort

"The man without the Spirit does not accept the things that come from the Spirit of God, for they are foolishness to him, and he cannot understand them, because they are spiritually discerned" (1 Corinthians 2:14).

From time to time as you seek the Lord by constant use of discerning prayer, you will hear a little voice accusing you of being a fanatic—or worse. It comes with the territory. When you find yourself accused of various "ridiculous" or "stupid" things because you are a maturing Christian, let 1 Corinthians 2:14 comfort you.

Before that day in 1974, I thought those three women were worse than fanatical; I thought they were either brainwashed or crazy. I scoffed at everything they taught; their ideas seemed simplistic, foolish.

But it was I who was foolish. It was I who had to be changed. I had a good mind but no spiritual discernment. As for the accusation of fanaticism, both the Law and Jesus taught that we must "love the Lord your God with all your heart and with all your soul and with all your mind and with all your strength" (Mark 12:30).

All of what you are, *all* of what you think, *all* of what you do—now *that's* fanaticism!

One of the sweetest promises in the Bible is found in 1 John 3:1: "How great is the love the Father has lavished on us, that we should be called children of God! And that is what we are! The reason the world does not know us is that it did not know him."

When the world does not know you, it is because He does. Lean back into His lavish love and be secure.

Discernment: Can We Go Too Far with This?

Can we go too far? Yes . . . and no.

In "The Road I Travel" (*Guideposts*, July 1997), writer Elizabeth "Tib" Sherrill shared a humorous incident about her own path in learning to find God's guidance. Tib recounted her first experience, forty years before, with people struggling to hear

God at all times. She invited a couple over for dinner and watched, amazed, as they rolled their eyes to the ceiling before partaking of any of the dishes being passed around the table.

"The wife dipped the serving spoon into the scalloped potatoes," Tib wrote, "lifted her eyes, then passed the dish along untouched. Her husband took a helping of potatoes, but after checking the ceiling, turned down the next dish: 'No peas.'"

Tib grew horrified that something was wrong with her cooking.

"So it went. Gravy, rolls, relish—till at last I understood. It wasn't the ceiling they were consulting; it was God. They were seeking His okay for every item of food."

Obviously if our method of seeking discernment causes someone discomfort, it could be too much. We will talk later about the need to learn to discern not only *what* we think or do, but also *how* and *when* and *where* to do it.

Practicing discernment is always too much if it becomes a legalistic form. If you find you are trying to please God in order to qualify for some blessing, or if discernment becomes just another checkpoint on the road to perfection and holiness, then it is too much. "Doing all the right things" can signal the old trap of trying to earn your salvation. We can never earn God's grace gift of eternal life. It is a gift from start to heaven (see Romans 11:6; Ephesians 2:5).

Discernment is not a "have-to," as fence-painting was for Tom Sawyer; it is a "get-to," as it became for his delighted friends. Having to practice discernment is legalism. Getting to is a joy, to me and to my Father. The kind of discernment in daily things that we are discussing here is not learned in order to get some specific reward from God. It is practiced as part of an obedient, expectant lifestyle that leads to a listening heart, a heart that will someday beat in perfect time with God's.

So, as we are taught from the book of Job, "Let us discern for ourselves what is right; let us learn together what is good" (Job 34:4).

We get to start with a renewed mind.

Once Over Lightly

Life in the Lord can be likened to a race. Discernment is one heat of that race. As we begin to run, we find the solid ground of God's scriptural premises and promises beneath our feet. He wants us to hear His voice. He will encourage us every step of the way. He will help us over the hurdles of testing what we hear. (More to come on this.) We will, at the last, be able to take every thought captive to obey Christ. We will be maturing, discerning children of God.

Your Turn to Discern

1. Test yourself: Is Christ Jesus alive in you? Do you know Him personally and not just as some wonderful but far-off God? Have you surrendered your whole life to Him?

If you are not sure about your answers to these questions, please make or reaffirm your commitment to Him right now. Consider writing a note with the day and time in your journal or on the margin of this page, because I guarantee that at some point down the road, a little voice is going to cause you to doubt that you have ever done this or that you have done it "right." Your note here can send that doubt scurrying in a hurry (see chapter 9).

2. Review once again where you stand in your attitude about the Bible. With an open heart, ask God. Give Him time to answer. He will.

3. Have you set your will to obey what the Lord tells you? The opposite of obedience is rebellion. Watch for this to rise up in you as you begin to seek and hear the Lord's voice for you. When it does, ask forgiveness and move on.

three

The Renewed Mind

The heart is deceitful above all things and beyond cure.

Jeremiah 17:9

For out of the heart come evil thoughts, murder. . . .

Matthew 15:19

You were alienated from God and were enemies in your minds.

Colossians 1:21

These ideas seemed incomprehensible to me when I first ran into them. *Man is basically good,* I thought. *He can trust his instincts. He can do right by following his conscience.* I balked at Scriptures that said every human is born essentially corrupt in thinking and understanding, and that out of that corruption we bring forth imperfect and untrue ideas.

What about it? Didn't God call us "very good" (Genesis 1:31)? When did we become His enemies? Why did we lose the ability to discern His voice? And how do we learn to hear it again?

In the Beginning . . .

When the world was new, man and woman lived in unblemished communion with God and all His creation. Adam and Eve heard God's voice perfectly. Angels were probably no surprise to them. They may even have had the ability to communicate with animals (see Genesis 3:1).

Human beings were the pinnacle of God's creation. With us God now had His companions, His children, His heirs. Yet even before He created us out of the matrix of His love, He knew He would lose us. God foreknew that once He gave us intellect and choice, as well as the freedom to use these as we chose, we would eventually turn away from His perfection. And we did.

Read Genesis 3. It tells of our fall, and concludes:

> The LORD God said, "The man has now become like one of us, knowing good and evil. He must not be allowed to reach out his hand and take also from the tree of life and eat, and live forever." So the LORD God banished him from the Garden of Eden to work the ground from which he had been taken. After he drove the man out, he placed on the east side of the Garden of Eden cherubim and a flaming sword flashing back and forth to guard the way to the tree of life.
>
> Genesis 3:22–24

These verses may suggest an enraged God pointing His finger, shouting, "Go!" and then slamming the doors of heaven behind us, leaving us lost and alone on earth forever. He would have had every right to do this. It would have seemed rational, in fact, to blow up the whole universe and start over. But a key to God's heart lies in the verse just before those given above. Genesis 3:21 reads, "The LORD God made garments of skin for Adam and his wife and clothed them."

This is no vengeful God banishing us in unending wrath; it is a heartsick Father, losing His children.

Think about it. Until this point all creatures lived in the center of God's will and love, faultless in discernment, perfect in communication with Him. There was no death or pain. Then mankind chose to disobey, and death came to all living things (see Romans 8:19–21). As perfect Judge, God had to exact punishment. Unholiness could not coexist with a holy God. Adam and Eve had to go.

Yet, as perfect Love, God suffered a desperately broken heart. He Himself became the first in history to spill blood, sacrificing an animal to make garments for Adam and Eve. Even as they stumbled out into the cold, His beloved children were clothed warmly in His love. Can you see the tears in God's eyes and feel the anguish in His heart as Adam and Eve left Eden and the cherubim with flaming sword took up their positions?

Praise God for His love! From before the foundation of the earth He had a plan to restore all that would be lost (see Ephesians 1:4). Because He knew from all time that we would lose our ability to communicate with Him, He also knew what He would do about it.

As the first step, He would give every human ever born the need and opportunity to know Him. "Since the creation of the world God's invisible qualities—his eternal power and divine nature—have been clearly seen, being understood from what has been made, so that men are without excuse" (Romans 1:20). "He has also set eternity in the hearts of men; yet they cannot fathom what God has done from beginning to end" (Ecclesiastes 3:11). This eternity in our hearts is what some call "a God-sized hole." No matter how much we possess in this world, we always have a space where only He fits.

As the next step to reconcile mankind to Himself, God would choose to reveal Himself to one childless old man and woman—Abraham and Sarah—and then to establish a nation through their descendants. Through Moses God would share His Law with this nation. He would also give these people prophets, thus revealing His ultimate plan: At some point He

Himself would enter history as a human being. Through the incarnation God's Son would serve as the sacrifice required for mankind to return to fellowship, and ultimately to eternal life, with the Father. God, the perfect Judge, would see His own Son's blood spilled, and it would free forever those who believe in that Son's sacrifice, bringing us back full cycle into communion with Him.

This much has been accomplished already. Next, Scripture tells us, once "every nation, tribe, people and language" (Revelation 7:9) have had every possibility of accepting this sacrifice on our behalf, His Son will return to earth and restore it as Eden. How incredibly perfect and complete His plan is; sometimes I can hardly wait!

The Renewed Mindset

The loss of Eden, however, meant that no one could hear or see God unless He chose to reveal Himself. The Law, a set of good and perfect rules, showed that no one could work his or her own way to God in heaven. No human could keep them all, and keeping any fewer than all meant certain hell. By the time Jesus came, even His beloved Jewish people had grown away from the Scriptures and were unable to grasp the truth (see John 12:40). Jew and Gentile alike were now spiritually blind.

Remember 1 Corinthians 2:14: "The man without the Spirit does not accept the things that come from the Spirit of God, for they are foolishness to him, and he cannot understand them, because they are spiritually discerned." This is the way you and I were before we became the Lord's, and why even now so many people we love and long to have share our faith simply cannot yet see it.

When Jesus comes to us, His Spirit enables us to see and hear again. "Therefore, if anyone is in Christ, he is a new creation; the old has gone, the new has come! All this is from

God, who reconciled us to himself through Christ" (2 Corinthians 5:17–18).

The goal of this new creation is stated in Ephesians:

> You were taught, with regard to your former way of life, to put off your old self, which is being corrupted by its deceitful desires; to be made new in the attitude of your minds; and to put on the new self, created to be like God in true righteousness and holiness.
>
> Ephesians 4:22–24

What does it mean that our minds are made new? It is not mystical brain surgery in which we go to sleep one night and wake up the next morning with a whole new set of attitudes and behaviors. (Oh, that it were that easy!) Nor is a renewed mind something we can do by ourselves. The verb tense in the Ephesians passage is passive—"to be made new." The implication in the Ephesians passage is interesting: We "were taught" and we are "to be *made* new."

Someone Else is going to enable it to happen.

The renewal of our minds is a lifelong process by which, through the Scriptures, we see and then ask for God's truths to replace ideas we thought were true before we knew Him. Some of our renewing will be done sovereignly by the Lord, either quickly or slowly. Most renewal will be done with our voluntary acquiescence and participation—but it will still be the work of His Holy Spirit. Remember, "It is God who works in you to will and to act according to his good purpose" (Philippians 2:13).

Taking every thought captive to the obedience of Christ is part of this renewal. Even here it is the Lord Himself who nudges us to want to discern, and then enables us to act on it. What a comfort!

Within days of the April afternoon when He came into my life, the Lord began the lifelong process of renovating my mind and heart. Truth from the Bible challenged and changed me in my deepest thoughts. It laid bare my actions and reactions. It made me cry out to be different.

I noticed that it all hinged on where I set my mind. "Those who live according to the sinful nature have their minds set on what that nature desires; but those who live in accordance with the Spirit have their minds set on what the Spirit desires" (Romans 8:5). I began to want what God wanted instead of what I wanted. This in itself was proof that the Holy Spirit was beginning to change me, and a critical step in the process of learning how to discern His voice.

The New Kingdom

Why do our minds have to be renewed? Renewal is necessary because in becoming the Lord's, we are moved from the kingdom of this world to the Kingdom of God. Although I will not see it with visible eyes until I die, I live in a new Kingdom. I need to have my heart and mind renewed—revised according to the new system. Its premises and priorities are very different from the ones I absorbed from this world. A few examples:

The Kingdom of Man	The Kingdom of God
Man and his fine mind are basically good and can solve all problems.	Man and his fine mind are no longer in touch with truth; everything he does and thinks is corrupted (see Matthew 15:11).
If I do enough good in life I can cancel out the bad I have done and go to heaven.	If I seek to save my own life, I will lose it. "Self" has no ability to save itself. No one can keep the Law or do enough good to earn eternity with a pure, holy God (see Matthew 16:25; Mark 8:35; Luke 9:24).
My worth is measured by status symbols, by good works that people can see or by what people think about me.	My worth is secure in God's love, and I am beloved by Him (see Ephesians 5:1).

(continued on next page)

The Kingdom of Man	The Kingdom of God
Those who do the biggest or best things are the greatest people.	Those who serve others most humbly are the greatest (see Matthew 23:11–12).
God helps those who help themselves.	God is the help of the helpless and hope of the hopeless, not of those who help themselves (see John 15:5).
If we cannot perceive it with our senses, it is not real. Tangible fact must come before faith: Show me God and I will believe!	Jesus said that anyone who has seen Him has seen the Father. Faith comes before fact; if I believe, then I will know (see John 14:9; Romans 1:17; 2 Corinthians 4:18).
Truth is relative, especially where God and faith are concerned.	Truth is absolute and eternal. The Word actually became flesh and lived among us as a Person so we could not just know Truth but see it in action (see John 14:6).

The differences in *modus operandi* between "the kingdoms of this world" and "the kingdoms of our Lord, and of his Christ" (Revelation 11:15, KJV) are endless. No wonder our minds have to be changed!

Being Sanctified

Renewal from the inside out is part of the process called sanctification. When I come to the Lord, I am, because of Jesus, sanctified—that is, set apart for God's use.

We are commanded to be holy because God is holy (see Leviticus 11:44). But for you and me to see this Christlikeness become reality in us means a lifelong process of purification. The process is specific for each one of us; no two people are conformed to His Word in the same way or order or pattern. The goal is the same, but the process, individual.

God knows you so intimately that He alone decides when to work on an area such as "loving" or "self" or "forgiveness" in your life and when to wait. You get to listen and then move with Him as He brings you into your unique wholeness.

During my first year in my new faith, friends gave me the titles of almost fifty Christian books that had helped them grow in their faith. I read most of them avidly—books such as *Something More* (Chosen, 1974) and *The Renewed Mind* (Bethany, 1974). But others I just could not get interested in. It was as if my brain fuzzed over when I looked at the pages. I put those away. Then, sometimes years later, one of those books would suddenly beckon to me from the shelf and, that time around, sing to my heart as I pored over the pages. It was God's time for that teaching.

Scripture is clear that all actions are outgrowths of attitude. Jesus said, for example, that if a man looks at a woman lustfully in his heart, he has already committed adultery with her (see Matthew 5:28). Jesus also said that these hearts of ours are essentially corrupt and cannot by themselves bring forth good attitudes (see Matthew 15:19). Before I can do good works, then—truly right and appropriate actions—I have to have a good, true, renewed heart attitude.

Most of the time for me, the process is slow. But sometimes my attitude changes so quickly and completely that I am unaware of it until later—when I am very grateful to learn of the change.

In the early 1970s I thought I was being a good mother. I read books with titles like *How to Raise a Brighter Child* and *Child Behavior* and applied many of the things I read. Yet on the inside my attitude was no different from the one by which I myself had been raised. "Children should be seen and not heard" was really my parenting goal. To me, as to my parents and to their parents, childhood seemed a waste of time; it was adulthood that had real meaning.

But after my April encounter with the Lord, my heart began to discern God's heart regarding children. I began to see my young sons as unique individuals. I saw the value of childhood. Jesus' words "Let the little children come to me" had new meaning: He loved them as they were. I began to hug, touch and snuggle my children more. I listened to them with both ears, respecting their uncertain phrasing, trying to hear what they were really saying. These new attitudes and impulses came automatically out of my joy-filled heart.

One night several months later I desperately needed a babysitter at the last minute. A bright, outspoken young woman, Chris Roediger had often babysat for us earlier on, and the boys and I loved her. But for some reason she was no longer available. No matter how much leeway I gave her, her schedule always seemed too full to take on the Rogers brood. Now, in my desperation, I called and begged Chris, and she relented grudgingly.

But suddenly, after that night, she was available to babysit for us again. Eventually she told me why.

"I stopped babysitting for you, Mrs. Rogers, because you had these three wonderful little boys and you treated them as though they hardly existed. I felt uncomfortable around you. But something has changed around here. Whatever it is, you treat them differently, and I like it!"

I am sure I smiled at Chris, but later that evening I had a good cry about the uncaring way I had been treating my sons. And how humiliating it was for someone to see how insensitive I had been when I thought I was doing a good job. But in a few minutes the Lord's warm love reminded me that He had already forgiven and started to renew me. Part of me rejoiced through my tears that the changes He was making were starting to show.

Slowly I, the former feminist, was rethinking my roles as wife and mother. I was learning the joy of being a biblical woman. Even without a career beyond "professional mother," I found I had a unique place in the universe. My quiet prayers, as I sat at my dining room table, could reach the heart of the King of the universe and actually change the world.

When I shared some of my new insights with an unbelieving friend, I found that the process of changing one's mindset is not always understood. I was growing in discernment; she thought I was being brainwashed.

Brainwashed or Washed Brain?

Everyone has an opinion about almost everything; and at some point everyone wants to convey an idea from his or her mind into the mind of someone else, and do it in such a way as to change that person's thinking. At its extreme this process is brainwashing. It reached its modern zenith during the Cold War years when Communists locked people up and played doctrine recordings 24 hours a day. Cults also use brainwashing techniques, cutting initiates off from friends and family, depriving them of proper nutrition and sleep and urging them to think, say and do only what the leader of the group says is right.

God wants to change our thinking, too, but not brainwash us. Scripture says that He yearns to "wash" our brains—to cleanse, heal and renew them from the world's false mindset. He does not want to leave us "mindless," but "mind-full," able to discern or recall His ideas and practice them in love. He wants to make us clean and move us beyond ourselves in service.

How does God wash our brains? Ephesians 5:25–26 gives a clue: "Christ loved the church and gave himself up for her to make her holy, cleansing her by the washing with water through the word." Just as the water of baptism symbolically cleanses us from the old flesh life, so the Word of God cleanses our minds, hearts, feelings, attitudes and, ultimately, our actions. Gently the Lord washes away years of grime in our thinking and replaces it with the truths found in His Word.

In April 1974 I knew next to nothing about the Bible; I could count on one hand the number of verses I could recall. Obviously I had to find some ways to work Scripture into my busy daily routine.

So I began buying records of Scripture in song and playing them as I did housework and cooked. I purchased the Bible on cassette tape for the car. I found a daily devotional composed exclusively of Scriptures centered on a daily topic and left it in the bathroom—the only place the mother of young sons has any quiet time!

On the rare days when Bill and the boys were gone for a few hours, I set up an in-house retreat. I placed a Bible and notebook on the dining room table, put my favorite Christian music on the stereo, and ran back and forth all day long between chores to sit for a few minutes to read, pray and listen for His voice.

From the first I asked God to show me how to find time every day to read the Bible and pray. I also asked Him to help me understand what I read. The times and methods have changed over the years, but He has always been faithful to answer this prayer, often in very creative ways. There have been long, wonderful seasons of group Bible study as well as study on my own.

By God's grace, 25 years down the road, I know I have been washed by Scripture every single day. This only pulls me on to more study and listening and obedience: The Holy Spirit has indeed changed my mindset. He has "washed my brain" in wonderful ways.

The Process of Renewal

I have found over the years that the process of renewing our mindset follows general patterns. I have also learned that once we have finished part or all of a process, the Lord may test us in it.

PATTERN 1: RENOVATION

As I write this, our house is being renovated. We have lived in it for fifteen years; it was long overdue for paint, carpet and dozens of major and minor repairs. I am thrilled at what is happening, but I hate the process. First come the estimates of time and money. Next, scheduling around our busy lives. Then, when our contractor arrives to paint or replace, things get totally torn up. He may finish one job or he may leave something partially done until another task is finished. At some point everything will be done and the house will be a delight to behold. In the meantime we live in varying degrees of mess and chaos.

This is much like what happens when the Lord renews a particular mindset. For me it usually begins when I hit a verse that makes me stop and think. I begin to relate it to one of my behavior patterns or ingrained reactions or attitudes. Often I start to feel resentment, anger or rebellion at the recognition that I need change. Sometimes for hours, sometimes for weeks, I try to ignore or rationalize my behavior or attitude. The interior of my "house" gets chaotic with conflicting thoughts. Convicted by the truth, but more out of guilt (more on this in a later chapter), I make a few stabs at trying to improve myself. But self-effort is always futile.

Soon I feel as if the renovation will never happen, that I will never be changed. Then I turn a corner. I see a verse in a new way or read something pertinent in a book or really hear something someone says. A friend calls these moments "little epiphanies." At last I lay down my rebellion and resentment and say, "Yes, Lord, have it Your way." Then the change begins to become evident, and at some point I know it is complete. I am renewed in that area of my thinking and behaving.

PATTERN 2: SHRAPNEL REMOVAL

We can relate a second pattern in the renewal process to what soldiers experience after taking shrapnel in a war. Sometimes years later these bits of metal work their way, one at a time, to the surface of the body. There they cause pain, inflammation, even infection. But the pieces can be removed, antibiotics applied and the sites freed to heal permanently.

This process is one God has used in my life to expose and heal painful childhood memories. He brings a buried memory to the surface. I feel the hurt all over again. The Holy Spirit encourages and enables me to apply the antibiotic of forgiveness, both given and received. Then He heals the site.

PATTERN 3: TESTS AND LAB SESSIONS

Sometimes after God has renewed our thinking in an area, He gives us a test or lab session in which we get to practice what we have learned. His purpose is at least twofold: to get us to affirm what He has taught us, regardless of the challenges, and to show us that we really are new in that area.

After three years of lessons on being a woman, wife and mother, I was given a magnificent, eighteen-year lab session—in the person of David, our fourth son—in which to practice and rejoice in the changes God had made in me. I loved this take-home exam! But some of my lessons produced tests I felt sure I was going to fail.

Like any good teacher, however, the Lord knows when His students are ready to pass a test. It might be difficult, and we might flounder for a bit, but ultimately we are able to respond in the way that brings an A+. Read Job; the whole book is a case study in faith-testing.

Rethinking Myself: An Example of Renewal

One of the major areas in which the Lord needed to renew my mindset was in the falsehoods I believed about myself. The Lord began teaching me new attitudes about myself. Many times it seemed I could not learn the lessons. But because of His faithfulness, I was given enough lab sessions in which to practice and rejoice in the changes He was making in me. The following example was one of the toughest.

THE PROBLEM AND THE PROCESS

The word *dysfunctional* was unknown as I grew up, but it describes my family perfectly. We were Mother, Father, First-born (me) and Son. True to the pattern of many dysfunctional families, one of us children was considered the "perfect" child who could do no wrong. The other was seen as the "scape-goat" who could do no right. Although research indicates that usually the firstborn is considered the perfect one, in our case my younger brother was given that role. I became the scape-goat. This position, coupled with a firstborn's sense of respon-sibility, devastated me. My childhood input from my parents and brother left me with the feeling that the problems we had were largely my fault, and that I had no value as a person. The bottom line of my attitude about myself came from my father.

"Roberta," he told me, "you are unlovable. No one will ever love you unless you change."

Whether he said it once or a hundred times, I believed my father's dictum implicitly from the first time I heard it. The problem was, I could never find the way to change myself for more than a few minutes at a time. That meant, I believed, that I would always be unlovable.

I reached adulthood emotionally scarred. On the surface I appeared a bright, well-adjusted woman. People often thought I knew more than I did. I gave an impression of competence that I did not feel. Recently I ran into Dr. Bob Haubrich, a for-mer college professor of mine who said, "I remember, Roberta, how you seemed to have a sense of how it all fit together." Yet during those years I felt like an awkward misfit—inferior, angry and frightened. Somewhere deep inside I had to have *some* value, didn't I?

During the first twelve years of my life in Jesus, He opened each self-concept and painful memory one by one. Generally He used the shrapnel process. A childhood memory—some event, perhaps, or something like my father's statement to me—

would rise to the surface of my consciousness. I would feel the hurt and rejection all over again. Then, gently, the Holy Spirit would talk to me about my pain and anger. He would often have me picture Jesus right there in the painful scene, loving me, hurting with me. He would use the laser of forgiveness to cut and cauterize. Then He would heal the memory, washing it with Scripture about how beloved I am and how He saw and loved me even "while I was being knit together in my mother's womb" (see Psalm 139:13).

Slowly my whole self-concept changed. I began to see myself as a child beloved by my Father God, infinitely precious and unique, a combination of saint and constantly-being-forgiven-sinner.

Now when one of those painful memories comes to mind, I find I am separated from it. It can no longer cause me any pain or stir up an ugly response in me. I find only the joy of having been renewed by the truth. After twelve years of gentle changing, God gave me a final exam in self-concept. He knew I was ready.

THE FINAL EXAM

It had been an incredible week. At my brother's instigation, our family had come together for counseling for the first time ever. Although Clark and I were in our forties and our parents in their seventies, I felt real hope for renewal. I left Bill and the boys at home and stayed at Clark's house, about two hours away, in order to be nearer to the meetings.

After the last session Clark and I were both numb emotionally from the intense few days. We talked about what had gone on. After some general conversation, he said somewhat heatedly, "Berta, you were a bit too honest with the counselor. You betrayed family secrets."

"I thought that's what we were there for," I responded. "To get it all out where it could be dealt with."

I tried to explain what I meant, but I could see his anger building. Suddenly he opened up with a barrage of criticism. His comments went on for several minutes.

"Frankly, Roberta," he concluded, "you are a fat, hypocritical Christian. I don't see any changes in you over all these years that would make me want to know your God!"

I was stunned to the core about how my brother perceived me, as a person and as a Christian. I could not respond.

After a sleepless night, I drove home the next morning in a daze, feeling dizzy, wondering if it mattered if I even reached there. I was pummeled by doubt. *How, after twelve years as a believer, could you have been so deceived into thinking you were growing up, growing better in the Lord? If your own brother sees no change in you, then has it all been a lie?*

Thoughts raced through my mind. I knew I should take them captive, lift them up to God. But I could not grab a single one. I was too numb.

Clark's words had resurrected my old self-concept. To me the implication was again clear: Unless I changed, I was still unlovable, worthless as a person and, even worse, as a Christian witness. But some of the things he had criticized, I knew I could not change. I felt like a lost child all over again.

"O God," I prayed, "I can't feel Your presence. Let Bill help me hear You. Let him be gentle, especially if all this is true. If Bill agrees with what Clark said, then I'll know I'm worthless. I just don't know what I can do about it."

For the two-hour drive I hung naked in some inner space, stripped of the ability to see who I was or who I should be.

When I pulled into the driveway, Bill came out to greet me. He perceived immediately that something had shaken me to my core. Slowly I climbed out of the car and we went into the house. Dropping onto the sofa, I took a deep breath.

"Clark said . . ." and I poured it all out. Finally I waited for Bill's response.

It came not as a bludgeon, but as soft, healing rain onto my soul.

"Honey," Bill said as he touched my hand gently, "I think both you and your brother were deeply upset. There might be some truth there, and you can accept that and learn from it. But mostly it's not true at all, or not true anymore."

Quietly, rationally, Bill helped me discern truth from falsehood. A few of the things my brother had said contained a grain of truth. Yes, I was a heavy person, as was my mother and her grandmother before me. It hurt to think that Clark could not see past the outer "me" to who I really was or was becoming. It also bothered me that my size could hinder my witness. I would (and did) talk those things over honestly with the Lord.

After a few minutes of Bill's calming words, I realized that most of my brother's words were only echoes of the same, negative statements I had heard as a child: *You are unlovable. It's all your fault.* My heavenly Father had long since labeled those concepts as not necessary to be believed.

When I was finally calm enough, words formed deep inside my heart: *Now it's time to choose, Roberta. You know what you have learned. What is the truth?*

That October afternoon I chose to believe only what God had told me about myself. I was beloved in His eyes. I had been and was being changed. All that had happened in the last twelve years was real. And I turned and walked away from my brother's words, forgiving him as I did so. I was indeed a renewed self—not perfect but at peace. I had passed my final exam in self-worth.

Although since that day I have struggled from time to time with feelings of rejection, never again have I had to go back to square one in the area of worth. "Set your minds on things above, not on earthly things. For you died, and your life is now hidden with Christ in God" (Colossians 3:2–3). Rethinking self is just one example of the myriad ways God renews our minds as He teaches us to discern what our thoughts are and where they come from. In the next chapter we will see what those thought sources might be.

Once Over Lightly

When man lived in Eden, he had perfect communication with God. He could learn the truth from the Source of all truth. When Eden was lost, we lost the ability to hear God's voice and to want to know and obey His truth. Our minds became corrupted by pride and by the visible world in which we now live. But God had a plan, and when that plan became a Person and lived among us, He gave us the desire and opportunity to be renewed.

As you and I give the Holy Spirit opportunity to work Scripture into us, He begins to wipe away old attitudes—about God, about ourselves, about others, about things that happen to us or what we are to do. We have come to this point in our lives with preconceptions about almost everything. Many of these ideas we have never lifted to the Lord to see if they are really true. Regardless of what we think we are, all our preconceptions will eventually come under the light of God's truth. The laser of His love will burn away whatever is not true, be it good or bad, and replace it with His own insight and value. He will begin to remold us into the image of Jesus, who never thought too little or too much about Himself.

As we read and think about Scripture and pray, the Lord will wash our minds, change our mindset and renew us in a never-ending process. We are learning to discern.

your turn to discern
Your Turn to Discern

1. Stop for a moment and think about *you*—who you are, where you live, what you do, how you define yourself, how you feel about your life. Think about what you have been taught about yourself. What are three generalizations you would use to describe yourself? (If these are primarily on the negative side, find three positive ones, too.)

2. Pray about these generalizations. Ask the Lord how He sees you. Does any Scripture come to mind? If not, use a concordance to look up passages about how God sees us, once we belong to Jesus Christ.

Here is a technique that blessed me: To see myself in a new way, I took advice from a pastor and sat down with a pad and pen to read the New Testament letters from Romans to Jude. I "received" each letter as if it had been written just to me. Anywhere the authors had written *you are* or *you have*, I wrote the verse out, changing the pronoun from *you* or *we* to *I*. Try it. And just wait until you hit the word *Beloved*!

3. As you look at your life in the Lord, have you seen Him change other preconceptions? Are there ideas you have held dear that you think He might want to change?

4. What ways can you find to work Scripture into your everyday lifestyle?

four

Discerning
the Source of Input

A key element in discernment is figuring out where our thoughts, ideas and feelings come from. Many theologians suggest four categories of input: *the world, the flesh, the devil* and *the Holy Spirit*. Because we process the world through the self, I have combined the world and the flesh, and will discuss in this chapter three major sources: *self, Satan* and *the Holy Spirit*.

Thoughts from the Holy Spirit are always true. Impulses from Satan we can reject immediately as lies. And ideas from the self need more in-depth testing, which we will cover in the next chapters.

Regardless of how many categories you recognize, if you can learn to discern the source of a thought, you are well on your way to finding out if an idea is from the Lord for you.

Source 1: Self

Self as I use it here includes everything in the world that has affected you from the moment you were conceived. It includes sensory input and how you processed it, the voices and words of your parents and siblings, teachers and leaders; the world philosophy in which you were raised or to which you were exposed over the years through courses, books, media. It includes your sin nature—the proclivity toward sinning and missing the mark that is part of our post-Eden makeup. Self is affected by your genes and your current emotional state and by what you ate for dinner last night.

Most of our thoughts come from this source—from the lives we live in our bodies in this world. Thoughts and feelings originating with us may or may not be true, no matter how firmly we feel or believe them. We are often our own worst enemies! As we saw in the preceding chapter, we come to the Lord needing renewal. In His perfect timing, He will reveal and help us rethink this source as He renews us, removing untrue ideas and replacing them with His truth.

What all does the *self* consist of? 1 Thessalonians 5:23 says: "May your whole *spirit, soul* and *body* be kept blameless at the coming of our Lord Jesus Christ" (emphasis added). Just as the reality of God is revealed to us in three Persons—Father, Son and Holy Spirit—so the self comprises three parts.

We are made up of *body*—the fleshly, genetic shell in which we live out our days; *soul*—the seat of our intellect, will and emotions (and, some would say, personality); and *spirit*—the spiritual facet that functionally died in the Garden of Eden and is reborn in us by the Holy Spirit when we put our trust in Jesus Christ.

Until we come to the Lord, we get used to looking at our bodies and souls and thinking that is all there is to us. But there is more.

THE BODY

Each of us arrives in life encased in what Paul and Peter both called a "tent" (see 2 Corinthians 5:1, 4; 2 Peter 1:13). We are a magnificent compendium of the genetic input of thousands of generations of people we do not know and a few we do. This body—very much part of who we are—also shelters the soul and spirit until at last we die and go to be with the Lord. He will give us new, eternal bodies.

In the meantime our earthly bodies give us ideas about who we think we are and, to some extent, who or what others think we are. Stereotypes are often based on someone's observation of our external shells. In the last chapter I spoke of my brother's stereotypic observation that if my body did not conform to a thinness standard, then my faith was invalid.

Stereotypes lie, and judging a person based on them will give us no true discernment.

THE SOUL

The soul—the seat of our intellect, will and emotions—is all the wonderful stuff that helps to make up *you*:

Your thinking abilities and processes
Your emotional makeup and feelings
Your conscience
Your will—that part of you that says yes or no
Your character and personality

We make decisions, entertain thoughts, feel emotions and determine actions—and learned reactions—in the soul.

The biblical idea of *soul* includes the concepts of *heart* and *mind*. Jesus stated that "the things that come out of the mouth come from the *heart*, and these make a man 'unclean.' For out of the heart come evil thoughts, murder, adultery, sexual immorality, theft, false testimony, slander" (Matthew 15:18–19, emphasis added). Why is this so? Because our post-Eden souls are fallen: "The *mind* of sinful man is death, . . . hostile to God. It does not submit to God's law, nor can it do so" (Romans 8:6–7, emphasis added).

Yet Jesus affirmed that our souls were actually created to glorify God. The goal of our existence is to "love the Lord your God with all your heart and with all your soul and with all your mind and with all your strength" (Mark 12:30). Your growing love for God is the ultimate renewal of your soul, accomplished not by you but by the Holy Spirit.

Romans 8:6 also says that "the mind controlled by the Spirit is life and peace." We talked in the previous chapter about the need to be renewed in our minds. What a wonderful outcome: *life* and *peace*, abiding life and indescribable inner peace for our souls. (We will talk about this peace in a moment, and again in chapter 6.)

WHAT ABOUT EMOTIONS?

In his *Confessions* St. Augustine wrote: "Man is a great mystery, O God. . . . His hairs are more easily counted than his feelings and the emotions of his heart."

We are used to thinking that the emotions rising out of our souls, which clamor so loudly to be heard, are telling us the truth. In our culture we use emotions to make the most important decisions of our lives. We choose our friends, make our enemies and select our mates based on how we feel about these individuals. But emotions, magnificent as they can be, are often no use in telling us what the Lord wants in a situation.

I say *often* because, as I will cover in detail in a later chapter, one "emotion" actually validates discernment for us. As Christians we can expect a special experience of peace—the indescribable inner peace for our souls that we just saw in Romans 8:6—to enable us to know when the Lord has spoken to us.

In chapter 7 I will cover a few emotional deceits, such as fear and doubt. In the meantime, think for a moment: The uglier emotions—for example, anger, hate, bitterness and jealousy—seldom originate with the Holy Spirit, and once we begin to allow them too much play, our enemy can inflame them beyond our control. Our nicer feelings may deceive us as well, being influenced by our observations or physical states. But these finer emotions, submitted to the Lord, can become God's marvelous icing on the cake of our renewed lives.

When the Lord reached me that April, for example, I was so unhappy in my marriage that I was considering separating from Bill. We were emotionally alienated and too busy to do anything about it. Then I read this in 1 Peter 1:22: "Love one another deeply, from the heart."

Without much hope of an answer, I tossed up a prayer: "Lord, I don't feel love for Bill anymore. So if You want me to love him again, You'll have to do it. I can't."

I agreed with the Lord that I would not leave Bill, and that I would choose to "love" him in actions, even if I did not have the feelings. At that point love became a decision.

Eight months later we stood side by side in front of our living room picture windows. The lights on the Christmas tree lit up the snow falling outside.

"You know, Bill," I said softly, "of all the miracles I've seen this year, I think the greatest one is loving you again."

As gently as the snow filling up the woods, God had added the emotion to my willingness. My feeling of love for Bill was restored, even enhanced. It was a gift from the Lord and doubly precious.

CAN'T I LET MY CONSCIENCE BE MY GUIDE?

The conscience is another part of the soul.

Recently our friend Derrill Ballenger, knowing I was working on this book, asked me some cogent questions.

"Is the conscience you carry from your childhood a voice from God?" he asked. "If you were raised by Christian parents, is theirs the voice of God? What about if you were *not* raised by Christian parents but were taught about right and wrong? Is that voice the voice of God? Notice how I just ask questions," he added, "and don't have any answers!"

As far as the conscience is concerned, I don't either, Derrill. In fact, where conscience is concerned, even the Bible is inconclusive. Paul refers to his own conscience as clear before God (see 1 Corinthians 4:4), but he also indicates that consciences can be "weak"—that is, unfit to judge truth (see 1 Corinthians 8:7, 10, 12).

But we can consider these thoughts.

When I was a child my mother took me to see the Disney film *Pinocchio*. I can still remember Jiminy Cricket's song adjuring me to "let your conscience be your guide." For me as an unbeliever, this might not have been a bad idea. It was at least some moral compass by which to make decisions.

But now that I am the Lord's, I have to lift up even this part of myself to be renewed. My conscience has been influenced by all those who have had input in my thinking. As Shakespeare wrote in *King Richard III*: "My conscience hath a thousand several tongues, / And every tongue brings in a several tale, / And every tale condemns me for a villain."

I can no longer follow Jiminy Cricket's advice. Now that I am a Christian, my guide is not some cultural and religious conglomeration of moral ideas inside my head, but a living Holy Spirit available to counsel and lead me into truth.

I can always listen to my renewed conscience when it nudges me to obey the Lord. I can sometimes ignore what used to be conscience when it comes at me with vague, finger-wagging guilt. Even of our consciences, then, we have to ask, "Is that You, Lord?"

THE SPIRIT

"She has real spirit!" we say when we like the attitudes and actions of someone facing a challenge. This may be true as one definition of *spirit*, but it is not the biblical concept. James 2:26 starts with: "As the body without the spirit is dead. . . ."

68

This may sound confusing, but remember that you are composed of three interconnected parts: a protecting body; a feeling, thinking soul; and a center core empowering your life. Our spirits were meant to be like the blazing, molten middle of the earth, providing constant renewal. Although we were created to be this way, however, we were born with this part of ourselves shriveled up, cold and useless. When we come to faith, the Holy Spirit gives birth to our spirits. Until then, strange as it sounds, because we are living in eternal separation from the Father, in whose image we were created, we are dead in the core of our beings, even though we walk around and think and eat. We are like flashlights without batteries.

Jesus told the intellectual Pharisee Nicodemus: "I tell you the truth, no one can enter the kingdom of God unless he is born of water and the Spirit. Flesh gives birth to flesh, but the Spirit gives birth to spirit" (John 3:5–6). Our true spirits are what died in Eden. My pastor friend Dale Becraft says, "To be dead in spirit is to be separated from God, with no ability to discern His voice or be in His presence."

When we choose to put our trust in Jesus Christ, the Lord's Spirit indwells us and becomes the radiant power center giving life and, ultimately, resurrection power to enable us to "bear the likeness" (1 Corinthians 15:49), both now and forever, of the Son. The Holy Spirit is the nuclear core of our spirits. As His power moves through us, we are drawn closer to Him and become more and more like Jesus.

Ultimately each of us who believe will be a complete, eternal unit of resurrected body, soul and spirit, just as Jesus was, who appeared to hundreds of His followers after His death, burial and resurrection (see Mark 16:19; Acts 1:3; 1 Corinthians 15:5–8). What a future!

Source 2: Satan

My friend Debbie Vahle and I were commiserating on the telephone. Well, actually, I was pouring out how frightened I was about a situation, and she was listening. Deb, knowing well that I was trying to find the peace of the Lord, finally interrupted me.

"Bobbi," she said, "whatever spirit is bothering you here, it sure ain't the *Holy* Spirit!"

I began to laugh.

Satan. Demons. Dark things we do not want to think about. My college psychology professors assured me that "there are no spooks." And the few theologians I had met up till then indicated that all those biblical references to demons and deliverance were using those terms to placate the uneducated minds of Jesus' time. Such concepts have been superseded, so they said, by science and the study of mental illness. Modern medical terminology had done away with the antiquated idea of evil and demons.

In the weeks after my April conversion, however, I learned quickly about the reality of the unseen world around me. I learned that I have an enemy who wants to keep me from knowing or loving the Lord. If he fails at that, he wants to keep me from growing in God's grace and love. He wants to disrupt my prayers and keep me from sharing with others the wonderful things that have happened to me. In short he wants to cripple and destroy my faith and the new life it brings to me and others.

I also learned that God has a wonderful "secret service" of even more powerful angels, whose primary task is to minister to me and to all believers. These angels are not to be ordered about by us or to be worshiped in any way (see Colossians 2:18). They are servants of God doing His bidding alone. Although sometimes they become visible (Hebrews 13:2 says "some people have entertained angels without knowing it"), this is only as God Himself determines. These angels stay obedient to Him at all times.

In recent years television programs such as "Touched by an Angel" have reawakened our thinking about unseen beings. As Christians we need to know what the Bible says about angels (Hebrews is especially helpful), and keep Scripture as the standard as we watch programs or read books about angels, in order to discern the truth or lies presented.

SATAN'S ORIGIN AND CHARACTER

If demons are real, where did they come from? How could a good God create something evil?

He didn't.

When God created the universe, He created two particular kinds of intelligent creatures—human beings and angels. He gave both the ability to think and the freedom to choose. In heaven and on earth, God wants no puppets. He desires creatures who choose freely and joyously to obey Him.

When mankind was banned from the Garden, we lost the ability to see these other beings on a regular basis. They can still see and interact with us, however. Angels, good and bad, do not seem bound by the laws of matter or the speed of light. They can inhabit humans or animals, and at times have control over behavior and speech. The prophet Balaam found his donkey speaking God's truth to him (see Numbers 22:21–33). Satan spoke to Eve from a snake and she was not startled by it (see Genesis 3). And in the New Testament Jesus recognized Satan's input in Peter's response to Him and rebuked him (see Matthew 16:22–23).

We also read that Jesus ordered a demon out of a boy who seemed to be having what we would diagnose as an epileptic seizure (see Matthew 17:14–18). Sometimes Jesus healed a disease; sometimes He delivered someone from a demonic stronghold. Jesus knew how to discern the cause of what He saw. Through His Holy Spirit in us, He still does.

Jesus affirmed, "I saw Satan fall like lightning from heaven" (Luke 10:18). Most scholars use two Old Testament passages, Ezekiel 28:12–17 and Isaiah 14:12–14, to describe the creation and fall of the glorious "guardian cherub" Lucifer. He was the angel given highest authority over planet earth. In both passages it is clear that Lucifer (or Satan) had the power to choose to obey or disobey the God who created him. In his pride he chose disobedience and lied to himself:

> "I will ascend to heaven; I will raise my throne above the stars of God; I will sit enthroned on the mount of assembly, on the utmost heights of the sacred mountain. I will ascend above the tops of the clouds; I will make myself like the Most High."
>
> Isaiah 14:13–14

There are five "I will's" in that one passage, every one of them an impossibility, a lie. God alone is God. But ever since his fall, Satan has been enticing us toward his own deceived sin, pitting pride and self-will—what *I* want—against what God wants for me. Satan started with Eve and that tantalizing hiss, "Did God *really* say . . . ?"

In discernment the important thing to remember about what might be Satan's voice is what Jesus said about him: "He was a murderer from the beginning, not holding to the truth, for there is no truth in him. When he lies, he speaks his native language, for he is a liar and the father of lies" (John 8:44).

Whatever Satan plants is a lie. If we discern that a thought is from this source, we can forget it, drop it, ignore it or rebuke it, and walk away. There is no truth there for us to deal with, no matter how strongly we perceive it or how rational it may seem. If we discern that we have had input from an unholy spirit, we can dismiss those thoughts at once. No matter how compelling, they are a lie. "For there is no truth in him. . . ."

CAN DEMONS AFFECT BELIEVERS?

It is true that demonic entities cannot own us once we belong to the Lord. But Scripture makes it clear that until the devil and his minions are thrown into the lake of fire (see Revelation 20:10), they are still allowed, for God's perfect reasons, to be here. And they do affect us.

How do they hassle us most effectively? They wage war on and in our minds! Remember our goal Scripture for all discernment: "We take captive every thought to make it obedient to Christ." This goal is from a passage about spiritual warfare—ferreting out and eliminating the enemy—from start to finish:

> For though we live in the world, we do not wage war as the world does. The weapons we fight with are not the weapons of the world. On the contrary, they have divine power to demolish strongholds. We demolish arguments and every pretension that sets itself up against the knowledge of God, and we take captive every thought to make it obedient to Christ.
> 2 Corinthians 10:3–5

The war for our thoughts, minds, attitudes and actions continues all our lives on earth.

As an example, let's look at a situation Jesus faces as He nears Jerusalem, facing crucifixion. Mark 8:31–32 states:

> He then began to teach them [the twelve disciples] that the Son of Man must suffer many things and be rejected by the elders, chief priests and teachers of the law, and that he must be killed and after three days rise again. He spoke plainly about this, and Peter took him aside and began to rebuke him.

Peter loves Jesus. The impulsive fisherman is ready to do all, give all, be all for his Lord. When he hears awful ideas coming out of Jesus' mouth, he is distraught. In anguish Peter pulls Jesus aside and begins to rebuke the Lord of glory.

The gospel writer does not tell us what Peter says, but it may be something like this: "Surely You couldn't have heard right, Lord! God would never do a thing like that, not to *You*. Crucifixion is hideous. How could He ever let You suffer like that? Besides, we need You here. You must be wrong. . . ."

Jesus looks over His shoulder and, seeing the other disciples watching, speaks boldly enough so they all hear:

"Get behind me, Satan!"

verse 33

Satan? Where is *Satan* in all this?

He must be there, invisible to the others, because Jesus speaks first directly to him. He tells him where to go—out of His sight (an alternate translation of this phrase).

Notice, Jesus is not calling Peter "Satan." Peter does not get out of Jesus' sight or leave the group. Nor is there any indication that the disciple slinks away in embarrassment or that he takes this part of Jesus' response to mean himself.

Well, then, what is Satan doing there? He is putting thoughts into—or inciting thoughts already in—Peter's head, thoughts Peter takes as his own, thoughts the source or context of which Peter does not stop to discern. Poor Peter is now wondering, *What happened? Why was I wrong?*

Jesus continues,

"You do not have in mind the things of God, but the things of men."

verse 33

This part of Jesus' response is directed at Peter and the disciples. It gives them and us a classic example of how Satan operates: "You are not thinking the way God does. You are thinking as humans do."

Peter was looking at God's thoughts from a human point of view. Satan came along and added to his thoughts, or incited those thoughts to action. The ideas sounded wise and caring as Peter heard them rush through his mind and out of his mouth. Yet Peter and the others knew, if still dimly, that Jesus was the Christ, Emmanuel, "God with us in the flesh." When

Jesus spoke, it was God speaking. They also knew the passage in Isaiah where God proclaimed,

> "My thoughts are not your thoughts, neither are your ways my ways. . . . As the heavens are higher than the earth, so are my ways higher than your ways and my thoughts than your thoughts."
>
> Isaiah 55:8–9

For some reason Peter forgot that God does not always make human sense. He did not want what he heard coming from Jesus to be true. He did not stop to discern. Knowing Scripture, cleansed by his faith in Jesus Christ (see John 13:10), talking with Jesus face to face, Peter found nevertheless that Satan was right there, unseen, planting thoughts in his head.

If Satan could do this to Peter in the presence of Jesus, you had better believe he can do it to us! This is why we must learn to trace out the sources of the ideas that come to us, and learn to "demolish arguments and every pretension that sets itself up against the knowledge of God, and . . . take captive every thought to make it obedient to Christ" (2 Corinthians 10:5).

Source 3: The Holy Spirit

The third source of input is the one we want to learn to hear above all others.

When you open the doors of your life to the Holy Spirit, He may come in like a rushing wind, blowing over everything in His path, as He did with me. Or He may come as a soft spring breeze wafting through the windows of your soul. But when you ask, He comes. And He alone knows the truth—in court vernacular, "the truth, the whole truth and nothing but the truth."

Who is the Holy Spirit? He *is* the Truth. He is the essence, the power, the living Presence of Jesus, who said, "I am the . . . Truth" (John 14:6). For two thousand years of Old Testament history, the Holy Spirit came as a special Anointer for individual men and women. He was sent forth by God to help in specific situations, to breathe into the writers of Scripture and to enable God's prophets to prophesy the future.

This changed with Jesus and the New Covenant. As He prepared to leave His disciples, Jesus said an incredible thing: "I tell you the truth: It is for your good that I am going away. Unless I go away, the Counselor will not come to you; but if I go, I will send him to you" (John 16:7). He also said, "You know him, for he lives with you and will be in you" (John 14:17).

Jesus, who stood before them, flesh and blood, loving them as only God could, would be *in* them by the power of the Holy Spirit. There is no more intimate way for God to relate to His children than to permeate their very beings. This is what Jesus made possible for all of us. The voice of the Spirit is no longer available just for a chosen few. Since Pentecost it is for every one of His precious children—for all of us who come to Him. The indwelling Holy Spirit is the voice of God. His is the only voice that knows all truth. It is this voice that we, as His children, must learn to hear and obey.

In the Bible God has given us practical tests and methods to help us discern whether a thought is His own for us. In the next two chapters we will learn some of these.

Once Over Lightly

As we learn to discern, we need to decipher which of three sources our thought or idea or emotion came from: self, Satan or Spirit (the Holy one!).

Thoughts from our soulful, sinful selves—from the worldview by which we were raised and in which we live—may or may not be true. These may contain some truth, but most of the time we can be dubious about launching out immediately to obey an idea or impulse if it comes from self.

Satan always lies; if he has planted an idea we have taken on as our own, we can rebuke and forget it.

Only the Holy Spirit knows all the truth all the time. It is His voice, His thoughts, not our own or Satan's, that we as Christians ultimately seek. We must learn to check the sources of our thoughts thoroughly, to take every thought captive to Christ.

Your Turn to Discern

1. Think about a specific problem or person or event you have faced today. (For example, a relative undergoing medical tests.)

2. What are you thinking or worrying about regarding this? (For example, *Does she have cancer? I wonder who her doctor is? How would I care for her if she is really sick, what with the kids and all?*)

3. Based on the three input sources, can you discern where these thoughts about your thoughts originated? (Probable sources: The first question above is from self with a nudge from Satan; hear the worry? The second question would be from your rational self. The third is a worry started in self and fueled by the enemy. A nudge to pray for her and the idea to help care for her . . . now that's the Holy Spirit!)

4. For the next few days practice grabbing and tracing your thoughts to the source. Ask the Lord to help you. He will.

five

Primary Tests

Once I knew why I had to test my thoughts, ideas, plans and emotions, my next prayer was, "O.K., God, let's get practical: How do I do this? Once I have zeroed in on my thought, what kinds of tests do I need in order to have Your clear direction in my everyday decisions?"

Some things became obvious right away. I knew, for instance, that any methods of testing would have to line up with the Bible. I soon realized that I would need tests to discern whether I should do something or not; to assess ideas before accepting or rejecting them; to decide whether or not I should speak or deal with someone at any given time.

Whew! It was beginning to sound complicated—taking my thoughts captive and then testing them. But the Holy Spirit reminded me that I was a learner, and that this learning would take time, and that the Lord has all the time in the world.

Well, over His time the Lord has indeed taught me various ways to check those captive thoughts for His will.

Most commonly I use some combination of the following five tests to check out my short- or long-term plans, as well as the thoughts and ideas that come to me:

1. The Scripture test
2. The test of time
3. The fruit test
4. Confirmation by circumstances or other persons
5. The order and priority test

In the next chapter we will look at what I call "pocket tests." These are tests we can carry with us as quick determiners. But the discernment received from all these tests, whether pocket tests or "primary" tests, must stand against three ultimate questions (two we will see in the next chapter): "Is it scriptural?"; "Is this loving?"; "Do I have the peace of God that passes understanding?" Loving others is the goal of, and peace is the fruit of, true discernment. Scripture is the bedrock of our faith and practice.

1. The Scripture Test

The first and ultimate question for every thought, idea, emotion or plan must be: "Is it scriptural?" If something is forbidden by Scripture, it must be rejected immediately. It is not from the Lord. He cannot contradict Himself.

Here is an easy example. Suppose someone tells you that Jesus is coming back at midnight on December 31. That information cannot be true because of what Jesus says in Matthew 24:36: "No one knows about that day or hour, not even the angels in heaven, nor the Son, but only the Father." End of argument.

Obviously the more Scripture we know, the faster we can test a thought to see if it might be God's voice speaking to us.

Within an hour of that moment when the Lord broke in on my life, I was on the phone calling my husband at work.

"Bill, I can't leave the boys, but would you please do me a favor? Would you stop by the bookstore and get me a copy of *The Living Bible*? I have a special reason I need it today."

That special reason was that suddenly I wanted a Bible I could understand easily. I was hungry to find out as much as I could, as fast as I could, about this God who had touched me.

Once I had that *Living Bible*, I was surprised to run into a problem of sorts. The verses did not "sing" to me as I had heard others say they did to them. I could read the words and understand the ideas, but something was missing. I had thought reading the Bible would be fun, but it was not even interesting, nor did it seem relevant to me.

So it was not long before I prayed, "Lord, I know You want me to read and understand and enjoy the Bible. Well, I'm reading it, but I don't see how it applies to me. I'm not excited about it, as some of my new Christian friends are. Would You please change this for me? I want to read and respond to the Scriptures the way You intended."

I think you can guess the outcome of that prayer.

I pored over that paraphrase for three or four months, grabbing up ideas about God and His Kingdom. By fall I wanted a translation that offered notes and references to related Scriptures. Soon I bought a paperback concordance. The next year I purchased a Bible commentary and dictionary. Eventually I added *The Amplified Bible*, a Hebrew-Greek interlinear Bible and another presenting the text in chronological order. I found a Scripture-only daily devotional and several "Bible promises" books and left them in places where I could snatch them up in a quiet moment. (Remember the suggestions for Bible time in chapter 3?)

When the computer age reached me, I installed a Bible program in my laptop. Now I have added to that alternate translations, a concordance . . . you see where this is headed!

The choices I made in building a small library might not apply to you—with the exception, of course, of owning a

Bible. You need one you can enjoy reading, one you feel free to highlight or underline, take notes in, fill up with prayers scribbled in the margins, watermark with tear stains. And you probably need to obtain a concordance if your Bible does not have one.

I have never been able to memorize whole passages of Scripture as some do, whom I greatly admire. Yet after years of daily exposure, the wealth, the pure gold, of Scripture is there for the Holy Spirit to call to mind. And He does. Using a concordance I can even find the location of passages in fairly short order.

Twenty-some years down the road, it still takes a choice on my part to open the Bible every day, but once there, the Holy Spirit almost always teaches, convicts, excites or comforts me in something I read.

Storing up Scripture by seeing or hearing it every day accelerates the process of learning to discern the voice of God. He will never tell you anything that violates Scripture or scriptural concepts. Test everything at the start and at the end by seeking Scripture about it.

Two Suggestions as You Read

In addition, here are two suggestions: Check the context and implications that come with a portion of Scripture.

1. Check the Context

If you think God has given you a verse that fits a particular situation, check the context of that Scripture to be sure you are accurate in your interpretation. The context is the whole historical or thematic setting into which the Scripture fits. The context does not have to involve the same situation you are facing, but make sure you understand the context and have extracted the idea accurately before you apply it. (I will give a specific example of how to check the context of a Bible passage in "Was Jesus a Vegetarian?" later in this chapter.)

2. CHECK THE IMPLICATIONS

Our thoughts must line up not only with what Scripture states, but also what it implies. Many verses contain obvious commands such as "Love one another" (John 13:34) or "Be my witnesses" (Acts 1:8), but our direction in discernment might not always be expressed in such succinct words.

In His parables, for example, Jesus gives us not direct commands but implied information, often about the nature of God the Father. The story of the Prodigal Son in Luke 15 is a clear illustration. Not only do we learn about God's incredible, forgiving love, but we learn about right and wrong responses through the two sons' reactions—all by reading between the lines.

A WORD OF CAUTION

The New Testament provides examples of religiously trained people not really hearing God in the very Scripture they espoused. In Matthew 22 Jesus is confronted by a group of Jewish Sadducees. They were the rationalists of the day; they accepted nothing "spiritual." For the Sadducees there was no spirit world, no immortal soul, no resurrection from the dead. They also denied the oral tradition of the Jews and clung tenaciously to the Law as set down by Moses. They were intensely scriptural.

The Sadducees did not like Jesus any better than the Pharisees did and wanted to trip Him up. So they pounced on Him with a law stating that if a man died, his brother should marry the widow and have children vicariously for the dead brother (see Deuteronomy 25:5). They gave Jesus an example of a woman who had run through all seven brothers in a family. Then they asked Him, "At the resurrection, whose wife will she be?" (Matthew 22:28).

His answer (that there would be no marriage relationship in heaven) was prefaced by this devastating statement: *"You*

are in error because you do not know the Scriptures or the power of God"
(verse 29, emphasis added).

Jesus said this to men who claimed they knew the Scriptures—and thus God—inside and out. Well, they knew the words, but they did not personally know the One who had inspired the words. They did not know either the depth of His knowledge about, or the minute care in His loving heart for, each of His creatures. They knew neither that the hairs of their heads were individually numbered nor that God was so personal and powerful that He wanted to be involved in how they understood and applied the Scriptures they thought they knew so well. They saw only the words and accepted only what their finite brains could reason out. They lacked spiritual discernment.

I have to be careful that I read the Bible and share its truths with this fiery statement of Jesus' in my heart and mind. I may not really *know* the Scriptures or the true power of God in a given situation. I may know a truth that I think will apply to someone. It may be very scriptural. But God is far more personal than His words on a printed page. He is intimately involved in the lives of His children. He knows what truth needs to be shared in what time and what way in order for the fruits of love, joy, peace, patience to be effective in the lives of both the sharer and the receiver of that truth.

I must know both the Scripture and the power of God.

2. The Test of Time

If you need a way to see if some doctrine or idea you are receiving is God's, it can be helpful to look at Church history and practice up to about 325 A.D.

During this time the Holy Spirit helped the early Christians recall all that Jesus had said while He was on earth (see John 14:26). Those are the years during which the New Testament books were written and codified. The Body of Christ still agrees on the basic creeds set down during these centuries.

If you are dubious about a group's ideas or you think you are being enticed by a cult, see how their teachings stack up against Church doctrine established in the first three centuries or so. If their creeds are in full agreement with the basics, they are most likely just fine. If the group has added to or taken away from the ultimate basic—that Jesus Christ came in the flesh as God's one and only atonement for mankind's sins, and that salvation comes only by individual faith in that atonement—then beware.

At the same time, do be aware that there are disputable matters allowed within the Body of Christ. The Bible acknowledges differences within the Body on nonessentials (see Romans 14:1) and tells us not to quarrel about them (see 2 Timothy 2:23–24). This is why we have so many denominations today, all of them adhering to the basics set up long ago but differing in some of the details. But within all churches, any person who believes in Jesus as his Savior and the only way to God is a Christian. He or she is my brother or sister. The Body of Christ is more than any one piece of it.

AN APPLICATION: WAS JESUS A VEGETARIAN?

Let's take these tests and apply them to a "Letters to the Editor" column in the *Washington Times*, February 6, 1998. The headline *Animal Rights Group Claims Christ Was a Vegetarian* appeared over a letter. Here is an excerpt:

> The Gospels presently included in the Bible have been changed markedly since they were first written. The earliest translations we have are from the fourth century and have undergone many changes and at least one language translation. Evidence indicates that the story of the loaves and fishes did not originally include fish . . . and Jesus, when He refers to the (multiplication) miracle, refers only to the bread (e.g., Matthew 16:9–10; Mark 8:19–20; John 6:26).

84

Later, referring to the extra food left after the feeding of the five thousand and the four thousand men, the letter-writer continued:

> From a practical standpoint, it is unlikely that travelers would carry dead fish in their baskets—which would spoil the bread and make them sick. Also, if Jesus were not a vegetarian, when the disciples asked how to feed the hungry masses, He could have simply pointed to the sea and told them to go fishing.

At the end of his letter the writer concludes:

> Christians should follow the compassionate Christ by being vegetarians. As we do to the least, we do to Him.

These claims, which may seem as confused and ludicrous to you as they do to me, do provide a clear example of how to test ideas we hear or read.

The first statement that the writer makes is about the ostensible changes in Scripture. Do you recall what the Bible says about that? Read John 10:35, 2 Timothy 3:16 and 2 Peter 1:20–21.

Next here's a good place to call on the test of time, or established Church doctrine. The letter-writer says that Scriptures "from the fourth century . . . have undergone many changes and at least one language translation." The writer is correct, which is why we might use the test of Church practice and doctrine *before* the middle of the fourth century. However, this test proves nothing here.

To further test the letter-writer's ideas, review the accounts of the feeding of the masses in Matthew 14:15–21, Mark 6:35–44 and John 6:5–13. Based on our early Church-established Scriptures, are fish part of the feeding miracles? Yes, they definitely are.

Now read the three passages the writer refers to in his letter—the ones in which he says fish are not mentioned by Jesus.

Is he right? Yes, fish are not mentioned in these references to the miraculous feedings. So, what do we do about that?

Look again at the context of Matthew 16:9–10, Mark 8:19–20 and John 6:26. Why doesn't Jesus mention fish when He refers later to the feedings? In Matthew 16:9–10 and Mark 8:19–20 the fish part of the miracle can be left out because the context of Jesus' reminder is an argument about bread only. And in John 6:26 Jesus is talking to an unbelieving crowd. Leaving fish in or out is not important to what Jesus is saying. Do these contexts prove anything either way as to whether fish were part of the miracles?

Look up *fish* in a concordance. You will find passages indicating not only that Jesus multiplied fish, but that He showed men where to catch them. He Himself, moreover, caught, cooked and gave His disciples one to eat as a sign to them that He was still alive after His death and resurrection (see John 21:9–14). Jesus was no vegetarian!

To see if Scripture has anything to say about foods that we as Christians should or should not eat, look up *meat* or *food* or *vegetables* in your concordance. Eventually you will come across Romans 14:2 and 1 Timothy 4:3. Romans says, "One man's faith allows him to eat everything, but another man, whose faith is weak, eats only vegetables." And 1 Timothy says: "[Hypocritical liars] forbid people to marry and order them to abstain from certain foods, which God created to be received with thanksgiving by those who believe and who know the truth."

But before you go off labeling Christian vegetarians as "faithless," run a context check. The Timothy passage condemns those who teach bad doctrine and practice, not those who eat or do not eat certain foods:

> The Spirit clearly says that in later times some will abandon the faith and follow deceiving spirits and things taught by demons. Such teachings come through hypocritical liars, whose consciences have been seared as with a hot iron. They forbid people to marry and order them to abstain from cer-

tain foods, which God created to be received with thanksgiving by those who believe and who know the truth. For everything God created is good, and nothing is to be rejected if it is received with thanksgiving, because it is consecrated by the word of God and prayer.

1 Timothy 4:1–5

The Romans passage does speak about Christians who have a need to follow certain rules:

Accept him whose faith is weak, without passing judgment on disputable matters. One man's faith allows him to eat everything, but another man, whose faith is weak, eats only vegetables. The man who eats everything must not look down on him who does not, and the man who does not eat everything must not condemn the man who does, for God has accepted him. Who are you to judge someone else's [i.e., God's] servant? To his own master he stands or falls. And he will stand, for the Lord is able to make him stand.

Romans 14:1–4

These in-context passages tell us why there is no need to be a vegetarian, but they also show us how to treat lovingly those Christians who may have dietary (or other) rules they want to follow.

Now we can look at the rest of the letter-writer's claims. First is his rationale about Jesus not giving people fish to carry away because they would stink. The little boy in the miracle carried fish *into* the site. People in that age were not stupid, as the writer assumes; they dried fish to transport it safely. The writer's explanation lacks common sense (a "pocket test" we will discuss in the next chapter).

Finally, check out in context the final Scripture in the letter, the one mentioning "as we do to the least." The reference is to Matthew 25:40: "The King will reply, 'I tell you the truth, whatever you did for one of the least of these brothers of mine, you did for me.'" In this powerful quote, who are "the least"?

Does it refer to animals at all? Can we in any way infer from this Scripture that we are to love animals as ourselves? I don't think so.

This letter-writer has a unique idea, but it is not scriptural by any test. His letter is full of confused human thinking. Jesus was not a vegetarian, nor do *we* have to be. The writer does not know, as we saw in the previous example, "the Scriptures or the power of God" (Matthew 22:29).

3. The Fruit Test

I use the fruit test in two situations: first, when I want to assess ideas I hear or read from a source outside the Bible; and second, when I am thinking about advising or helping someone.

In Matthew 7 Jesus' disciples asked how they could discern truth from error. He gave them the first use for the fruit test.

PART 1: LOOK AT THE MESSENGER

"Watch out for false prophets. They come to you in sheep's clothing, but inwardly they are ferocious wolves. By their fruit you will recognize them."

Matthew 7:15–16

Jesus was teaching His followers how to spot false prophets—those who would come bringing untrue ideas to them. He wanted His disciples to look first at the source of the ideas. Did the prophets' lifestyle bear fruit—that is, were they trying to match the goals God had set up in Scripture? Were the messengers generally humble, submitted to God, loving and faithful to their wives and families, kind, loving their brothers and sisters in the Lord and sharing what they had with others (see 1 Timothy 3:2–12)? A dichotomy between what they were saying and how they were living could indicate right off the bat that their teachings were not pure or true.

In that *Washington Times* letter on vegetarianism, if you skipped to the bottom of the letter first, you would see the writer signing himself as the head of an animal rights group. We know his bias before we begin to read his words—one more reason to be sure to test his claims.

PART 2: LOOK AT THE PROBABLE OUTCOME

There is more to the fruit test than looking at the messenger. We need to look at the fruit that doing or saying something might bring to our lives or to that of our hearer, and prayerfully assess the probable outcome.

Let's say I see a problem in a person's life or in our relationship. I really want to help and I think I know how to solve it. But not every situation that confronts me is dealt with specifically in Scripture. And just knowing I ought to say or do *something* is not enough. God is so loving toward us that He wants us to know the right time and the right way to share the right thing. Ecclesiastes 8:5–6 promises that "the wise heart will know the proper time and procedure. For there is a proper time and procedure for every matter." If we ask, the Lord will give us wise hearts.

Here's an example. Sometimes after we become believers, we have a tremendous desire to share what we have found with anyone and everyone we meet. While the desire to share the Gospel is scriptural, we need to be sure our personal lives are coming into conformity with the character of Jesus, and that we know whether it is the right moment in our hearers' lives to receive the good news we bear. Insensitive or dogmatic or legalistic sharing may actually drive the people we care about away from the Lord.

So we can use a fruit test to look at the possible result of our timing and of the ideas we share with someone. As far as we can tell, will our sharing right now produce good fruit in that person's life and in our relationship? Galatians 5:22–23 speaks about this kind of fruit: "The fruit of the Spirit is love, joy, peace, patience, kindness, goodness, faithfulness, gentleness and self-control." And James 3:17 describes "the wisdom that comes from heaven" as "full of . . . good fruit."

For me, looking back at the feminism I espoused so strongly in my twenties, I see clearly that the fruit of it was, and would only be, dissatisfaction and selfishness. No matter how I applied the well-meant but distinctly human ideas of my militant feminist comrades, they were not going to bring love, joy, peace, patience, kindness or goodness to my life or to the lives of my family. In me the fruit was bitter—anger, dissension, hurt.

But I need more than just a rational assessment of what the fruit might be. I need insight. Because I cannot see into the lives and hearts of my hearers, I must pray and wait for the Holy Spirit to nudge me for when and what and how to share. And then obey!

Job's comforters and my own life both offer examples of how the fruit of a thought or action should be discerned ahead of time.

JOB'S COMFORTERS

Job sat in the ashes of his life. He had lost the children he dearly loved; he had lost his livelihood; and now his health was gone. All he had left was a very unhelpful wife and three friends who came to "sympathize with him and comfort him" (Job 2:11). They told Job great and wonderful things about God, all of which were basically true. They also told Job that if he would only do this or that, or say this or that, or confess this or that sin, then God would get him out of the situation that his own sinfulness had put him in.

The three friends may have had the right idea—that Job would discern his own sinfulness. But:

> After the LORD had said these things to Job, he said to Eliphaz the Temanite, "I am angry with you and your two friends, because you have not spoken of me what is right, as my servant Job has. . . . My servant Job will pray for you, and I will

accept his prayer and not deal with you according to your folly. You have not spoken of me what is right, as my servant Job has."

Job 42:7–8

When God twice says, "You have not spoken of me what is right," does that contradict the statements the friends made about God? No. God was angry because of what those men did with their truths (although the words they spoke about God were true). God had not sent those circumstances as a punishment for Job's sins, as his friends had implied. He had sent them as a test of Job's faith. God was angry because what those men did with their "truths" was not true for Job in his specific situation.

They came to comfort Job but forgot to run a fruit test. Each man should have first remembered the fruit of Job's life— that he honored God, prayed for his family and was kind to the poor (see Job 4:2–4). Before each one spoke, he should have asked God, "Will this truth about You that I am sharing bring comfort to Job? Will I be able to give it gently and kindly, or will it sound harsh to him? Will it give him the desire and ability to change, if he needs to, or only add to the awful burden he is carrying at the moment? Is my own heart motivated by Your loving Spirit, or do I just want to be 'right'?"

Their failure to discern not just what to say, but when and how to say it, added to their friend's anguish and made God angry with them.

In My Own Life

For four years, as my husband worked afternoons and evenings, the bulk of raising our four young sons fell to me. Disciplining them became my biggest problem. Whenever I thought to stop and ask, God helped me discern the right thing to do and the way to do it.

One of the four boys, for example, has a voice (inherited from me) that can be heard six city blocks away. His childhood bellow could be deafening, even when there was no urgency or anger behind it. Peter needed to learn the truth that "a gentle answer turns away wrath" (Proverbs 15:1), because his loud requests begat an equally loud response inside me.

I prayed about what to do. Soon I took to ignoring Peter—at least for a moment or two—as he informed me and half the Western world that it was snack time and that he wanted a cookie.

Once I was sure I was in control of my anger or tiredness and frustration (the beam in my own eye), I found myself kneeling down and turning his face to mine. Then I said in a quiet, evenly modulated voice, "Peter, it's O.K. for you to want a cookie. It's cookie time. But I can't hear you when you ask so loudly. It sounds like a demand to me. I can only hear you when you ask in a quieter, politer voice."

And I went back to changing David's diaper or getting dinner or whatever I was doing. When Peter was able to ask in a quieter voice, he got his cookie.

I had truth to share with this son, but first my own attitude had to be clear and I had to hear God's timing and way of dealing with the problem. I had to make sure the fruit would not be increased tension and anger and vocal escalation between Peter and me, and that our basic bond of love would not be broken.

In time this worked. And God had a plan for that voice! Pete's life now is spent shouting commands over the roar of aircraft engines.

The fruit test is not just having the right thing to say, as Job's comforters and I did; it is also seeking God's voice to know if and when and where and how to say it. The fruit test is like a series of traffic lights. If any of them is red, we must stop. If any is flashing yellow, we must be cautious and wait for further instruction. If they are all green, we can proceed. God's methods are consistent with His entire nature. Loving edification ("building up") is always both the goal and the way to get to it. The fruit for the sharer and the hearer must be sweet.

4. Confirmation by Circumstances or Other Persons

The confirmation test is especially helpful when you are choosing an action or deciding on a long-term plan.

To *confirm* means "to verify, strengthen or establish." Sometimes when you are seeking God's guidance, He will confirm His plan through circumstances or other people. In fact, when you are facing a life-changing decision, it is best to ask God to confirm it through Scripture (in addition to the Scripture test) as well as through others and circumstances.

Confirmations come when the Lord makes sure you read or hear or experience things that relate to your situation. You will perceive them as His confirmations, however coincidental they seem to others. For days in a row, for example, you may read or hear the same Scripture or various Scriptures that relate directly to your situation. Or you may hear a snatch of conversation or a story similar to what you are experiencing.

Your commitment to follow this decision will remain strong when Satan comes knocking to convince you that you are wrong. God can confirm your choice by natural or supernatural events.

NATURAL CONFIRMATION: A NEW CAREER

Some years ago our friend Royal Farris was a pastoral counselor in Texas. In his heart a dream was growing. He wanted to oversee a new kind of home group ministry in a church somewhere, and pass on his scriptural counseling skills to church members. He hoped that as they shared the Gospel with their neighbors, they could then minister in their own homes to those who needed reconciliation and healing as they grew in the Christian life.

One night Royal awoke and found ideas of a job description running clearly through his mind. He got up and jotted down the phrases, tucking the paper away.

More than a year later, the week after his mother gave him an online computer service as a gift, Royal was surfing Christian websites on the Internet when he spied a small ad from a church in Maryland seeking an assistant pastor. When Royal flew north to meet with the senior pastor, he was given a written job description containing the same ideas he had received that night, worded in the way he had written them down months before.

It was one of several means by which God confirmed that this job and move were His plans for Royal and his family at that time.

SUPERNATURAL CONFIRMATION: GIDEON

Have you heard the phrase *fleecing the Lord?* "Fleecing" is another way of seeking confirmation of a plan. In prayer you throw all the details of your situation into the Lord's lap and ask for a special sign. "Fleecing" comes from the wonderful story of Gideon in Judges 6.

You probably remember how it began. One day out of the blue, the angel of the Lord appeared to Gideon and asked him to tear down the altars to Baal. Gideon was scared silly. He tried making excuses as to why he was the last person to do this.

As always when God has chosen a person to act for Him, He listened politely, then refused to accept the excuses. But He did a mighty miracle for Gideon to prove that the King of the universe was indeed speaking to him. That night, terrified to be seen, but even more afraid of God, Gideon destroyed the Baal-worship sites.

Then God spoke to Gideon again. This time He wanted him to lead the Israelites to a great victory. In spite of the powerful act God had just done, Gideon was still terribly timid and short on faith. He said to the Lord,

> "Look, I will place a wool fleece on the threshing floor. If there is dew only on the fleece and all the ground is dry, then I will know that you will save Israel by my hand, as you said." And that is what happened. Gideon rose early the next day; he squeezed the fleece and wrung out the dew—a bowlful of water.
>
> Then Gideon said to God: "Do not be angry with me. Let me make just one more request. Allow me one more test with the fleece. This time make the fleece dry and the ground covered with dew." That night God did so. Only the fleece was dry; all the ground was covered with dew.
>
> Judges 6:37–40

Can we still "fleece the Lord" for confirmation today? In his autobiography *Just As I Am* (HarperCollins, 1997), evangelist Billy Graham wrote about the 1949 crusade in Los Angeles:

> Should the Campaign be extended? . . . We needed a clear sense of direction from the Lord. [We] . . . prayed together over and over again as the last week wore on. At last we decided to follow the example of Gideon in the Old Testament and put out a fleece, asking God to give us a decisive sign of His purpose.
>
> p. 172

God answered this fleece with a miraculous phone call. But a week later Billy and his team were again wondering whether to close or extend.

> In our uncertainty about what to do, we agreed that the best thing was to put out the fleece again, as Gideon had done,

and ask the Lord for another sign. We were relatively inexperienced young men with a lot to learn.

p. 174

Again the Lord answered with a miracle only He could have orchestrated, and the campaign was extended.

As Billy Graham mentioned, often we do put out a fleece when we are in the early stages of learning to discern. As we grow in hearing His voice, we may need this confirmation less and less. But it is still available.

The wonderful thing is that nowhere in the Scriptures do I hear the Lord sighing in disgust over Gideon's (or Billy Graham's!) weak-faith requests. I hear only His love and encouragement as His children struggle to learn to discern His voice.

CONFIRMATION FROM PRAYING FRIENDS

If you are blessed with a prayer partner or church or fellowship that intercedes, it is always wise to ask them to pray for confirmation of something you feel is God's will. Just be sure you wait for that confirmation before you launch out. It will come. And if there is no confirmation, then start over to seek God's plan. Be patient. He will help you find it.

Confirmation will give you confidence and courage in a time of testing—or, as I call it in chapter 10, "the great wait."

5. The Order and Priority Test

One way to check whether something you want to do is the Lord's idea is to run it through the order and priority test. We need to see if we are out of balance somewhere along the line.

God loves order. He created a universe hung together in the unseen power of His love. Planets, stars, solar systems are all flung out in abundance, moving in perfect concert toward the end God has in mind. Pattern, plan, order—everywhere we see it.

My friend Jeanie Montgomery loves to make cloth flowers. To imitate a daffodil, she carefully dismantled a real one. Petal by petal, crown by crown, segment by segment, gently she pulled the sections apart. She found that the daffodil was made up of groups of threes and sixes, and the threes were grouped in twos, making sixes. Perfect order in such glorious beauty!

The Bible says that the order and pattern of nature and the universe provide proof of God: "Since the creation of the world God's invisible qualities—his eternal power and divine nature—have been clearly seen, being understood from what has been made, so that men are without excuse" (Romans 1:20).

God loves order in relationships, too. At various places in letters to the young churches, Paul and Peter established the concepts and attitudes of working order within the Body of Christ (see 1 Corinthians 12:25; Hebrews 13:7); within the family (see 1 Corinthians 7:2–5, 10–16; Ephesians 5:22–6:4; 1 Peter 3:1–7); and within the workplace (see Ephesians 6:5–9). They also wrote of our relationships outside the Body of Christ, with unbelievers (see 1 Thessalonians 4:12). These men knew that order, like obedience, brings to us the best blessings of God—among them, open communication with and discernment from Him.

Many excellent books have been written on the Scripture-based roles of husbands and wives and children, of men and women, of church attendees and leaders. As you read them, do so with loving discernment; the same rules apply to testing the ideas of Christian writers (including this one) as they do to everything else. Only Scripture is infallible.

Priority—ranking things by importance—is a corollary of order. Some Bible teachers start with God at the top of the list and rank a person's roles down through "family" and "church" to "community" and so on. While this can be helpful to keep in mind when we make certain decisions, it is the balancing of these priorities that is most important.

Once you have grasped the idea of balancing order and priority, you can use them to discern whether you have heard from the Lord.

DISCERNING PRIORITIES

Bob Compendium was a type A. He had boundless energy and loved to help people. He worked all day and served on church and community committees several evenings a week. At least one weekend a month he was busy with a church or volunteer project. Bob often told his wife and three small children that he loved them, usually as he tore out the door after a quick supper on his way to the evening's meeting. He knew Linda and the kids understood how important his church work was. At least he thought he did—until he came home one evening to find the house empty. Linda and the kids had moved to her mother's.

Everything Bob was doing—his day job, his church committees and volunteer work—was good. But just doing good did not mean it was God's plan for him. Bob had lost sight of God's balance in order and priority as he rushed from one place to another.

With some biblical counseling, Bob learned that he needed to ask God about many of the activities he had assumed were just fine. He learned that God has priorities for a person's life, and although focuses such as God, family, work, church, friends and community do not exact equal time or energy, there must be a clear balance of all.

Once Bob saw that his thinking had become jumbled, and that his priorities were out of balance, he was able to ask Linda's forgiveness. He cleared his extracurricular slate and started over, seeking God's specific wisdom, as well as input and confirmation from Linda, for each task he added. Peace, born of order, settled into their home once again.

But There Are Exceptions!

Usually God's plans for you do not depart from the balance of His general order and priority. If they do, He will confirm the exception, as He did for us.

In 1978 our family prayed and received clear confirmation that Bill was to accept a new job in Virginia. But once we got to Newport News, it looked as if we could not have heard the Lord correctly. Bill's new job meant he was pretty much unavailable during the boys' waking hours.

I have already described the wisdom God gave me as I sought Him for four years while Bill worked afternoons and evenings. But when this situation first came about, I was far from calm. In fact, I had to pray through tears of frustration. "Lord, this job is not helping Your order in our home. The boys never see their father, and I am left doing it all. Are You sure this is Your plan for us? It doesn't match up with Scripture, as far as I can see. Surely You would never have given Bill a job that would preclude his being here as husband and father."

My prayer was honest, and so was God's strong, deep answer in my heart. In His wonderful way, He reminded me of the confirmations we had already received. He gave me peace that this was His plan for this particular family at this particular time. And He let me know that He would fill the holes where Bill could not be father and I could not be both mother and father.

For the next four years God did just that. Whenever Bill *had* to be around for some reason, circumstances made sure he was. Prayer by prayer God helped us solve the problems of a family lifestyle that seemed to be out of order. Best of all He helped us adopt an attitude that enabled the boys to accept this unusually ordered life as what God had for us just then, and they displayed no signs of "dad deprivation."

If you are facing a situation that seems out of order, pray out your questions and problems one at a time. Ask God if this is His plan for your unique life at this time. If He says *Yes*, accept in peace and trust that He will fill all your unusual needs.

Testing for the balance of order and priority in your life can be a way to hear God's voice. And facing an occasional exception to what we think is His order can help draw us even closer to Him as we discern from Him all the details of our lives.

Once Over Lightly

Before you take action, run your ideas through some tests. See if the idea, the method and the timing are all scriptural. If pertinent, check out Church history on it.

Assess as best you can what the fruit of any action you take might be—in your life and in the lives of the others involved. Seek confirmation, both from the Lord and from others. See if your plan is balanced within God's order for your own life at this time.

As we will see in chapters ahead, sometimes even after running all the tests you know, you will still either have to choose to wait some more or, as my friend Mary Belote says, "Close your eyes . . . and jump." It is our heart and willing obedience the Lord wants, not our always being right.

Before you leap, however, the next chapter has a few quick "pocket tests" you can run.

Your Turn to Discern

1. How is Bible reading for you? A chore you have to do rather than an assignment you want to do? Do you have trouble finding verses that come alive for you? If you discern truth here, why don't you tell God? Ask Him to change your attitude and your ability to read and find life in His Word. (He will!)

2. Have you ever had a Job's comforter—or been one? Are you aware of ever having used Scripture in a way that left someone feeling hurt or vaguely guilty but impotent to change anything? Has someone treated you this way when you were going through a hard or incomprehensible time? If so, forgive or seek forgiveness. Ask the Lord how He wants you to comfort someone and pray that your comforters will have His true wisdom and comfort for you and others.

3. How is the balance of order and priority in your life? Even if you feel it is fine, be sure to look honestly at the fruit in your spouse, your children, your friends, your co-workers—the lives of those closest to you. This will give you the best assessment.

Suggestion: The next time you are hurt or offended by your spouse or a friend, ask God for a scriptural idea with which to explain your reaction. Then ask Him to show you any beam in your own eye in that area (see Matthew 7:3–5). Finally ask Him to pick the time, the place and the words to share the hurt or offense with the other person. If you do this in humility before God and wait for His answers, in short or long order, I promise that you will like the fruit!

Pocket Tests

A *"pocket test" is a question* I can ask when I need help making a quick decision. It is a small, portable tool tucked into a "pocket" of my mind to help me be sure that I hear the Lord. Here are nine of my pocket-test questions:

1. Is fear lurking somewhere in this decision?
2. Am I confused about any aspect of this?
3. Is this a "have-to" or a "get-to"?
4. Does it build up or divide the Body of Christ?
5. Will I feel guilty if I don't do it?
6. Does it make sense?
7. Am I being tempted or encouraged?
8. Will it pass the "love" test?
9. Is the peace of Christ present?

Yes or *no* answers to these questions can bring me to a halt or encourage me to move forward with confidence. Let's look at them one by one.

1. Is Fear Lurking Somewhere in This Decision?

Fear always lies. We will cover this in a later chapter, but for now consider this: If I can see clearly that the fruit of doing or not doing something will be fear or worry, then I know to stop and do nothing until I have the Lord's peace. At this point I will not act out of fear, or in spite of it.

The Lord speaks in and with peace. He does not speak in or with fear. Once I have the peace that empowers, however, I can walk over any fear that remains and move ahead. The main thing to remember now is that the Lord is not speaking to us in fear. I will have to wait and run other tests to see if this is something the Lord wants.

2. Am I Confused about Any Aspect of This?

If there is any confusion about an action I am considering, I must wait for God's peace and order in my spirit. "God is not a God of confusion but of peace" (1 Corinthians 14:33, NASB). Also remember Ecclesiastes 8:5–6: "The wise heart will know the proper time and procedure. For there is a proper time and procedure for every matter."

An acquaintance from a church we attended years ago had that wise heart and waited to do something until confusion became clarity. It had been a financially tight year for us as Bill changed jobs. As Christmas approached I saw a huge gap between my planned budget and my actual funds.

"Lord," I prayed, "I need about $150 to get through the holidays."

One morning just a few days later, this woman from church called and asked if she could stop by. Our congregation was large and I knew her only slightly, so I was delighted to have a chance to sweep the Legos and piles of laundry off the couch and prepare for a chat.

But when she arrived she seemed ill at ease. Finally she blurted out, "Uh, you don't know me very well, and nothing like this has ever happened to me before. I don't know if you have any needs or not, but, well, I know the Lord wants me to do this. Please don't be offended. I have tried to ignore these thoughts for many days, but they kept getting louder. I knew this morning that I would have no peace until I did this. We've had a good year in our business, so don't worry about the amount."

Pausing for breath, she handed me an envelope. Inside was $160, the amount I had prayed for—plus something to tithe. I burst into tears as I shared my need and recent prayer with her.

She had waited until her confusion became conviction, and from that came the proper timing for both of us to be delighted by what the Lord had done.

We will see more examples of how perfectly the Lord can move us to do something in the chapter, "Nudges and Knowings."

3. Is This a "Have-to" or a "Get-to"?

"Having to" or "getting to" is the difference between legalism and freedom in the Lord. If my feet are dragging, I need to discern whether it is my own reluctance or God pulling me back by the armpits. I need to wait until I am ready to do whatever it is in God's peace and strength and joy, regardless of my personal feelings.

Sometimes God will change your reluctance; sometimes He will use it to stop you from doing what He does not want you to do. You will have to discern which is which. Either way it is good to check out your attitude to see if legalism has crept in. Legalism says, regarding tithing or mutual submission or anything God asks, "I'm doing this, God, because according to Your Word I have to. But when I do, You owe me one!" Willing obedience says, "Hey, I don't know if I want to do this or not, but I believe You want me to, so stop me if I'm wrong."

Legalism tries to earn its way to heaven, both before and after salvation. But as my pastor, Brent Brooks, says, "We no longer have to jump through hoops." Paul wrote, "Through Christ Jesus the law of the Spirit of life set me free from the law of sin and death" (Romans 8:2). I do not *have to* do good things anymore; I *get to.*

4. Does It Build Up or Divide the Body of Christ?

This pocket test is one I use when I am reading or listening to something by another Christian. It helps me discern whether or not I should accept his or her ideas as godly teaching.

The closer I get to understanding the Lord's heart, the more I agonize when I hear one Christian tear down the denomination, church, ministry, method or doctrine of another. Scripture makes it clear that it is my job to love my brothers and sisters, to encourage and pray for them. If they stray from Scripture, I am to lead them back gently into truth, provided that the opportunity is given me and that I have made sure I am not making the same error (see Matthew 18:15–17; Galatians 6:1; 2 Timothy 2:5; Hebrews 5:2; James 5:19–20).

Thus I feel a real check in my spirit at language that tears down or belittles the working out of faith of any church or brother or sister in Christ. The Holy Spirit seeks to edify— literally, to build a building of—all of us. He wants to bring us into unity on the foundation of Jesus Christ. Jesus Himself prayed deeply for unity. Teaching cannot be from Him, therefore, if it contains a sniping attack on a member of His Body.

Charles Stanley wrote in *A Touch of His Freedom* (Zondervan, 1991):

> When it comes to disputable matters, we were never appointed to be one another's judge. We are free to disagree, but

we are never free to criticize. To judge others for their opinion on "disputable matters" is to take upon ourselves a role God reserves exclusively for His Son.

When I read or hear ideas that tear down (judge) rather than build up the Body of Christ over something not basic to our mutual faith, I ask for more discernment before accepting them. And I apply the same test to my own sharing: Am I building up the Lord's Body?

5. Will I Feel Guilty if I Don't Do It?

In chapter 9 we will deal in more detail with vague guilt, but here is our pocket test: Am I being driven by guilt in this decision? Doing something simply because I will feel guilty if I do *not* do it is not good discernment.

Make no mistake, the Lord does convict us of sin and we do feel guilty. But that conviction is a specific sense of guilt for having done a specific wrong, and with it comes a sense of His forgiveness, ready and waiting. True conviction is coupled with an expectant, encouraging attitude that helps us confess, receive forgiveness and want to be changed.

Vague guilt, on the other hand, is most often from our enemy, there to keep us in bondage to whatever we did or think we did. It keeps us from accepting forgiveness and from moving on in new strength. In *Lose the Weight of the World* (New Leaf, 1997), Charles Blair has written a wonderfully helpful section entitled "The Weight of Guilt." If you struggle with being unable to feel forgiven, I highly recommend it.

Let's look at an example. Suppose your church needs nursery workers. You have prayed about it and are uncertain. Your natural inclination is to work with older children, but you feel guiltier and guiltier each Sunday as appeals are made for help.

This is not true conviction nor the proper basis on which to make a decision about whether to work in the nursery. Find another test that will help you come to peace about it. If it really is a nudge from the Lord, it will not come with a vague sense of guilt attached if you do not do it.

6. Does It Make Sense?

As we discussed earlier, our own intuition and intellect are not always the best indicators that we are discerning the Lord's will. Common sense is a wonderful gift from God. The book of Proverbs indicates clearly that wisdom—God-enhanced common sense—should guide our lives. Yet, like the conscience, common sense can be tricked by the world or the enemy and needs to be submitted to the Lord.

As Hannah Whitall Smith (1832–1911) wrote in *The Christian's Secret of a Happy Life,* "We are not to depend on our unenlightened human understanding—but we are to involve our human judgment and common sense enlightened by the Spirit of God." When you are about to make a fast decision, ask yourself, *Does this make sense?* Many times the Lord will use this question to stop you from forging on ahead of Him.

Occasionally, however, He wants you to lay aside your own common sense for His "uncommon" one. Again, you will have to discern which is which.

Let's use this as an example. You have a sudden urge to take out some savings and send it to a missionary whose name has come to mind or whose material you have just read. You are on a tight budget or fixed income, and the idea does not seem to line up with common sense. Is it the Lord? It might be and it might not. Ask Him, "This idea sounds like a right thing to do, but it doesn't seem sensible to me. Is it from You, Lord?"

Give Him time to answer fully, and wait for "the peace of God, which transcends all understanding" (Philippians 4:7) before you act on or reject the idea. *If you get no other answer, go with the common sense*—or, in this case, reject the idea. If you get direction to do it, however, move ahead.

107

My journals chronicle numerous times that I found myself worrying more and more about how to stretch my household budget. Each time, as my worry grew, so did a recurring thought: *Give some more away.*

The first time I heard this, it did not make any sense to me. How could giving away more of what little money I had be legitimate guidance? But I ran all the tests and finally realized it was the Lord speaking to me. So I sat down and took a stack of requests from various Christian agencies and ministries. Into each envelope I put a dollar or two—all I could manage at the time. With every envelope my worry grew less.

After a few years of going through this cycle periodically, and each time realizing that giving more away lessened my worry, I got the hint. Now I laugh to myself and am not surprised to find that I am discerning correctly: When I get worried again about not having enough money, it seems it is time to give some more away!

Common sense is a great thing, but it needs to be submitted to an even greater God.

7. Am I Being Tempted or Encouraged?

Temptation is always with us. James wrote that "each one is tempted when, by his own evil desire, he is dragged away and enticed. Then, after desire has conceived, it gives birth to sin; and sin, when it is full-grown, gives birth to death" (James 1:14–15).

We all know what temptation feels like. It tugs at you, pulling you along, often with the compulsive *I must do/have this*. We can usually recognize major temptations, but there are smaller, everyday temptations, too. We have to learn to discern them as well.

God does not tempt us; He encourages us. You know encouragement. It is that "Hey, I can do this and do it reasonably well!" feeling. It has no compulsive edge. You feel confident, enabled, competent. I often have to run this test when I am shopping. Virtually every time I see something I like, I am simply being tempted.

But then there was the weekend Bill was gone to Ohio and I was wandering through Sears. I found myself looking at laptop computers. We had a desktop computer at home, but with two of us writing, our schedules often conflicted. Suddenly I found myself fingering a keyboard. Nice. The reach was right. I looked at the pricetag. Not nearly as high as some of the others, but still way out of my budget.

"That one was taken out by a young woman and returned after a few days," the clerk said.

I nodded as I ran my fingers over the soft keys one last time. Soon afterward I left the store. But on my way home, the idea of buying that computer grew and grew. Was I being tempted—or encouraged? It seemed ridiculous for me, the non-computer-literate one in the family, to go out and buy a computer without Bill's input. Ridiculous to think of such an expensive purchase at all.

Lord, if this is You, I prayed, *then show me how. If it isn't, then please take this silly desire away.*

The next day I went back to Sears and bought the computer. Why? Well, in between, I had read up on laptop computers, looked at consumer ratings and checked out the brand name, warranties and service. And while I was praying about it, the Lord reminded me that a beloved aunt had left me some stock. If I sold half of it, I could pay for the computer in full. I would still have some of her legacy, as well as an item I know she would have loved to have given me as a gift. (Wonderfully, the stock later split and I ended up with the same number of shares!) The peace I had was complete; it was tempered with joy. I knew it was the right thing to do.

When Bill arrived home from Ohio, he was flabbergasted that I had done something so uncharacteristic. But when he saw "Pooter" (on which I wrote this book) and heard about my prayers and research and payment method, he was delighted.

Take time to discern whether you are being tempted or encouraged. If you are being tempted, it is not the *Holy* Spirit.

8. Will It Pass the "Love" Test?

I have left the two most important tests for last: love and peace.

Love is the fruit that should ripen in the life of anyone involved with our actions. And peace is the fruit that should grow deep inside us as we find the Lord's will.

First, love. Am I aligned with God's best pattern for love? Is my attitude toward the other person involved in the decision one of respect? Will my doing or sharing this idea fulfill Scriptures such as 1 Corinthians 13 and Philippians 4:8? These passages tell me to think of the very best, the most loving, the most worthy things about a person, and then act out of that context of *agape*—unconditional love. Sincere love from the heart is always our goal, in every relationship, in all we do.

I am a confrontational person and need this test often. Inching my car up the crowded parcel pickup lane at the supermarket, for example, I can feel my lips tightening. *Will those bag-loaders see that it is my turn, or will they serve that van that just pulled in before they load my car?* Nothing makes me angry faster than service people who do not serve or who are not fair. Since it is not fair to let me sit when it is "my" turn and another person has cut in front of me, I have been apt to bark at the person loading my car. We are both fuming as I drive off.

Slowly, however, the Lord is teaching me a new way to react. I find myself praying as I sit in line. And I wonder about those baggers: How has their day gone? What problems do they face? When they finally show up to load my groceries, I may or may not point out that they, as "bagging professionals," are not fair to serve someone first who has cut in line.

And when I do not even bother to tell them, then I have learned a lesson in patience and in laying down my selfish needs in forgiveness.

You will find the love test most useful for clarifying your attitude toward someone and for assessing the probable outcome of your action in his or her life. It may not always be useful for deciding whether you *should* speak or act. This is especially true if you react differently from confronters like me—if you dislike rocking the boat and prefer peace at any price. For you it may be too easy to hide behind Scripture when action is called for, and to do nothing "in the name of love." If you identify with this, you need to discern some more before you decide to *avoid* sharing. Both of us need to ask the Lord, "How do You want me to speak the truth in love?" (see Ephesians 4:15).

Ask yourself: Is this the best way to show love for the other person? When I discern correctly, God's peace replaces my tension. Kindness banishes anger. Love wins.

9. Is the Peace of Christ Present?

This test undergirds everything. Peace sounds like an emotion but really is not. I have found, as I shared in chapter 4, that my emotions are often not a good indicator of truth. But the peace Jesus talks about is not a feeling conjured up by our selves, our inner digestive states or by circumstances that please us. It is something altogether different.

Right after He told the disciples about the Holy Spirit, who would come and lead them into all truth, Jesus said, "Peace I leave with you; my peace I give you. I do not give to you as the world gives" (John 14:27).

Over the centuries the idea of peace has come, to most people, to mean an absence of war, or perhaps inner quietness. But Jesus was clearly not talking about those definitions. He was emphatic that the peace about which He spoke is not "as the world gives." It is not about a cessation of military activity or stillness borne out of meditation, nor is it something created by us or by our circumstances. Rather it is something given *to* us.

The Greek word used for *peace* in the John 14 passage is *eirene*. *Strong's Concordance* says it probably came from a primitive verb *eiro*, meaning "to join." We translate the idea as the one word, *peace*, but the Greek implies "well-being, oneness, quietness, rest." It also connotes the idea of "to set at one again." This peace is a quiet sense of being joined together with God, of being restored and made whole by His power.

Jesus was a Jew and would have used the Hebrew word for *peace, shalom,* meaning "safe, well, happy, friendly" and the ideas of "welfare, health, prosperity, peace." This word suggests perfect peace, favor, prosperity, rest, safety, welfare—being wholly well. *Shalom* is well-being in body, soul and spirit.

Now think of these Greek and Hebrew concepts together in one ball and you have an inkling of what Jesus was talking about. This is important, because coming to recognize this peace is the bottom line of assurance that you are hearing the Lord's voice. The Shepherd of your soul speaks ultimately with this peace that He alone, by the Holy Spirit, gives.

If you have experienced the "peace of God, which transcends all understanding" (Philippians 4:7), you know how hard it is to describe, but you also know it is real. It comes with a "gut-deep knowing" combined with a filled-up sense of quiet well-being—an emotion you can never manufacture yourself. It settles down over and all through you, giving you a sense of being made whole, being made one (in mind or attitude) with God. You feel complete, confident, undergirded by the power of the Holy Spirit.

"At its core," says my pastor friend Dale Becraft, "it is a peace with God that allows us to remain secure and quiet in the inner man, no matter what may be transpiring. Remember Jesus sleeping in the boat in Luke 8, at total peace with His Father, while the disciples were in chaos and confusion?"

There is no adequate way to describe this peace, but I know it is real. Satan cannot reproduce it. It is the bottom line in hearing God's voice. Once we have run every other discerning test, the final one is this: "Is the peace of Christ present?"

We need to check Scripture and the love test aspect for the idea, method and timing of anything we do. Then, if peace is there for us and love will be demonstrated to anyone else involved, we can move ahead in confidence, regardless of what the world or our minds or the enemy throws at us. We have heard God's voice.

Once Over Lightly

Pocket tests are questions to ask in discerning the origin of ideas or thoughts. They are especially applicable when you think you ought to take some action and want to be sure it is the Lord's idea. James 3:17 gives us the best review. It offers a synopsis of what God's plan will look like when we discern it: "The wisdom that comes from heaven is first of all pure; then peace-loving, considerate, submissive, full of mercy and good fruit, impartial and sincere." We will be acting not out of legalism but out of sincerity. Nor will we feel fear or confusion or vague guilt. The Lord's plan will edify or encourage the Body of Christ. Ultimately it will be the best love we can give someone and will fill us up with the peace that passes understanding.

Your Turn to Discern

1. What pocket tests have you found that help you hear God's voice in everyday situations?

2. Have you ever experienced "the peace that passes understanding"? How would you describe it to someone who has not yet known it?

3. Why is the love test the best one to use in relationship questions? Can you think of a situation that would have been handled better if you or the other person had used it?

4. Colossians 2 contains some tests Paul recommends to help you evaluate an ideology. Can you see the warnings against humanism, legalism and asceticism? What other ideas do you discern in this passage?

seven

Falling and Failing

More Space for Grace

This chapter deals with our incredible failures and God's even more incredible grace. Adam and Eve, Jonah, David and others like them provide some of our best examples.

Jonah teaches us not how to discern—he had no problem hearing the Lord!—but what happens when we fail or rebel against what we know is the Lord's will.

> The word of the LORD came to Jonah son of Amittai: "Go to the great city of Nineveh and preach against it, because its wickedness has come up before me."
>
> Jonah 1:1–2

Whether God hollered in his ear, whispered in his heart or appeared in a dream, Jonah bar Amittai clearly heard from the Lord. But Jonah did not like what he heard. For one thing,

Nineveh was the capital of the Gentile nation Assyria. Jonah felt that the Assyrians should not be infringing on the rights and privileges God had given the Hebrews. Second, Jonah did not give a hoot about preaching to pagans who hated his country; he would rather they suffer the consequences of their wickedness.

So Jonah decided to avoid God's command. He ran. You know the story. He found a ship headed for Tarshish, the end of the known world, and booked passage. En route such a fierce storm buffeted the boat that the crew figured someone must have angered one of the gods to bring down such wrath. Jonah confessed that he was indeed a Hebrew running from the Lord, "the God of heaven, who made the sea and the land" (Jonah 1:9), and had himself tossed overboard. As every Sunday school child knows, Jonah spent three days and nights inside the belly of a great fish.

Here we get a glimpse of why God chose to work with this man. With time to pray and discern the Lord's voice, Jonah saw his errors. He worshiped his God and prayed, believing in His power and grace: "I, with a song of thanksgiving, will sacrifice to you. What I have vowed I will make good. Salvation comes from the LORD" (Jonah 2:9). And on the third day he was vomited up alive onto the sand.

The next time Jonah heard the Lord's command, he went to Nineveh and warned the people about their wickedness so powerfully that a revival broke out in that pagan city, and the residents cried out to God in repentance. They were spared annihilation.

Jonah, however, had another lesson to learn. Miffed at God's forgiving love toward those he still felt were unworthy, he sat out in the desert sun and pouted. God caused a gourd vine to grow up to protect him, and then withered it. At that point the Lord addressed him:

> God said to Jonah, "Do you have a right to be angry about the vine?"

"I do," he said. "I am angry enough to die."

But the LORD said, "You have been concerned about this vine, though you did not tend it or make it grow. It sprang up overnight and died overnight. But Nineveh has more than a hundred and twenty thousand people who cannot tell their right hand from their left, and many cattle as well. Should I not be concerned about that great city?"

Jonah 4:9–11

Whether Jonah ever heard with his heart as well as he discerned with his ears, we do not know. The story ends there. But how much we can learn from it!

Whether we fail to obey the direction we get through discernment or fail to discern God's voice in the first place we, like Jonah, will find that God will help us deal with our failures.

Learning from Jonah

We learn about both ourselves and the Lord when we look at the book of Jonah.

LEARNING ABOUT OURSELVES

As you practice hearing the Lord's voice in everyday situations, there will come times when you miss it or mistake it or forget to ask for it. It will also happen that you hear the Lord and simply do not want to obey. Either the timing will not be convenient, or the direction will not make sense, or you just do not want to do what He tells you. You will hear and choose to ignore it, or you will actually run in the opposite direction, as Jonah did.

What happens when you realize you have failed an opportunity to hear and obey the Lord, either by chance or by choice? As my friend Angela Dion laughs, "God may put you in a fish!" Yes, indeed, for a while you may find yourself in darkness. But, as Jonah discovered, when you confess, you find God's grace. This becomes a wonderful teaching tool as we let Him lead us gently into obedience.

LEARNING ABOUT GOD

When Jonah chose deliberately to disobey the word of the Lord, God could have wiped him out or shoved him aside and found someone else. I think I would have. But our God is not that way. He knows us individually, loves us intimately and knows what it will take to break or bend us to His wonderful will for our lives. Instead of annihilation when we fail, God chooses to offer us grace—the undeserved opportunity to repent and be changed.

This grace is a bottomless sea filled with His forgiveness. We can fail limitless times, even in the same sin, and when we turn in heart repentance to Him, still find all the love and forgiveness we need. How do we know this? Jesus told us that we must forgive someone "seventy times seven" (Matthew 18:22, KJV), which many Bible scholars say is a Hebrew concept for infinity. If we fallible humans are to forgive an infinite number of times, we can be assured that God's grace level is even higher!

Jonah went into a terrifying place inside the sea, and even there God's grace captured and delivered him from his own bad choice to run. Later, when Jonah was pouting, God spoke conversationally with him, encouraging Jonah to see things from His divine perspective. God's personal, loving grace is there for us in exactly the same way.

In the book of Jonah, moreover, we see God's compassionate grace not just toward one wayward Hebrew, but toward a boatload of unbelievers and a large city of wicked pagans. Once Jonah was tossed overboard, the sea calmed and the ship's crew worshiped the living God. When Jonah shared God's warning of destruction with Nineveh, that city experienced incredible revival. Its residents sat in sackcloth and ashes, symbolizing their repentance and desire to be changed. In His grace God did not destroy them.

Seven hundred years later Jesus confirmed the reality of Jonah and the fish and Nineveh's repentance (see Matthew 12:39–41; 16:4; Luke 11:29–32). Jesus affirmed that God's grace was at work in the repentance of the people, covering their sin. We know God forgave Jonah's sin because he received another chance. And Jesus Himself became God's grace cover for our own failure.

Fear of failure runs deep in us because, at its base, it touches our mortality. Somewhere in the heart of every person, Christian or not, lurks the sense that if we fail, we will die and go to hell. There are two grains of truth in this idea: one, not one of us will ever do enough good to outweigh our failures; and two, our failure to believe in Jesus Christ as God's way into eternal life *will* keep us on the path to hell. We are all on that path until we come to know Christ. Then we are saved; we are safe. Christians no longer need to fear our failures. We cannot die and go to hell.

Whether you miss the Lord by accident, by neglect or by deliberate choice, you will always find Him waiting for you. He longs for you to come and talk to Him and receive forgiveness. You will never out-sin His grace. You are safe to fail.

Reacting to Failure

Since we are safe to fail, what do we do when we find we have not discerned or obeyed correctly? Here are five suggestions.

1. DON'T HIDE

What was the first thing Adam and Eve did when they realized they had failed? They hid. They were afraid to look at God's face. They could not bear the light of His love in the face of their choice to sin.

119

But where can you hide from God? The Holy Spirit lives in you. The Lord lives around you. In fact, as Paul put it (quoting a Greek poet), "In him we live and move and have our being" (Acts 17:28). Romans 8:38–39 assures us that absolutely nothing can keep us from the love of God. Even running, as Jonah did, will not work. We cannot outrun God's loving presence. The psalmist wrote:

> Where can I go from your Spirit? Where can I flee from your presence? If I go up to the heavens, you are there; if I make my bed in the depths, you are there. If I rise on the wings of the dawn, if I settle on the far side of the sea, even there your hand will guide me, your right hand will hold me fast. If I say, "Surely the darkness will hide me and the light become night around me," even the darkness will not be dark to you; the night will shine like the day, for darkness is as light to you.
>
> Psalm 139:7–12

Do not hide your failure from God or yourself. Talk it over with Him. Do not be afraid to let Him love you, even when you are ashamed of or mad at yourself.

2. CONFESS

Confess means "to say with." When we confess our wrongdoing, we are agreeing with God, who already knows what we have done. Let's look at Adam and Eve's next sin: They hid some more—this time behind excuses. Oh, indirectly they confessed; they admitted they had done the deed. But they tried to justify why they had done it. "The woman you put here with me," said Adam, "she gave me some fruit from the tree, and I ate it" (Genesis 3:12).

Adam was blaming not only his wife but the One who made her! He was not really agreeing with God that he had sinned and needed to change. Confession is not making excuses for our behavior; it is going straight to God with the whole truth and nothing but the truth. Yes, that is humbling. But it is in the death of pride that the Lord can reach in and cleanse us.

Look at King David's confession after allowing himself to believe that he actually had a man killed so he could have his wife: "Then David said to Nathan, 'I have sinned against the LORD'" (2 Samuel 12:13).

David realized in horror that he had sinned against the Most High God, the One who metes out life and death. Yet Nathan replied, "The LORD has taken away your sin. You are not going to die" (verse 13).

Because of Jesus, we can follow the injunction of the writer of Hebrews: "Let us then approach the throne of grace with confidence, so that we may receive mercy and find grace to help us in our time of need" (Hebrews 4:16). This mercy and grace are there in any and every need we face, especially in the need to be forgiven.

If you have missed the Lord, confess honestly. No excuses.

3. RECEIVE FORGIVENESS

The blood of Jesus, his Son, purifies us from all sin. If we claim to be without sin, we deceive ourselves and the truth is not in us. If we confess our sins, he is faithful and just and will forgive us our sins and purify us from all unrighteousness.

1 John 1:7–9

John reminds us not to lie to ourselves. We are not to pretend we are innocent or that our mess-up (sin!) regarding our discernment was too small to bother with. It also tells us unequivocally that the Lord wants to and will forgive us, and that He will purify us from *all* our unrighteousness, large and small.

I remember the relief I felt the first time I heard this question: "For which one of your sins *didn't* Jesus die?" I still stop to think about that. The answer, of course, is, "None of them." He died for them all.

4. KEEP SHORT ACCOUNTS

Learning to discern in real life, every day, gives us many chances to grow in the knowledge of God's forgiving grace. We can use our small failures to practice big lessons. One of the biggest forgiveness lessons in the Kingdom is sometimes called "keeping short accounts." This means we take Ephesians 4:26 literally: "Do not let the sun go down while you are still angry." In fact, we can take this as wise counsel for any sin we have committed, not just unrighteous anger.

A good way to approach it is to think of cleaning out pipelines. Just as a liquid cannot flow freely through a pipe clogged with sludge, so it is hard for the Lord's messages to come through lines of communication that are impeded by sin. Let Him clear out every bit of muck from your life. Seek, give, receive forgiveness. Get cleaned out from past sin. Then, every day, with every specific failure that the Lord brings to mind, confess it. Talk it over with Him. Agree that you do not want to miss Him or ignore Him. When you are clean, the pure liquid of His love and presence can flow freely through your life. Recall the praise that flowed from Jonah deep in darkness in the sea (see Jonah 2:9).

Notice that we are talking here about failure *that the Lord brings to mind.* As we will see in chapters ahead, the enemy loves to drag us down with vague guilt. He would love to have you confess and then still feel guilty all day and all night.

Learn to discern which voice is God's loving, edifying conviction of sin and which is the enemy's guilt-ridden counterfeit. You can tell by the fruit, once you have confessed. If you feel cleansed and new, ready to try again, it was the Lord convicting you of sin. If you still feel guilty and tired or depressed or mad at yourself, it is most likely our old enemy dragging you down. Ignore him. You *are* clean and new again.

One of the most cleansing prayers in the Bible is David's Psalm 51—the one he wrote after being convicted of his dual sins of murder and adultery:

Create in me a pure heart, O God, and renew a steadfast spirit within me. Do not cast me from your presence or take your Holy Spirit from me. Restore to me the joy of your salvation and grant me a willing spirit, to sustain me.

Psalm 51:10–12

Pray it whenever you need to. The Lord will always answer.

5. GIVE GOD TIME TO CHANGE YOU

Sin is serious to God. But when it is forgiven, it is totally gone. Then it is O.K. for you to let go of both the sin and your guilt about it. The Lord has taken it away and forgotten it. Jonah got another chance to obey the Lord, and there is no record that he hung his head and said he was not worthy. He was no longer in the sea but his sins were: "You will again have compassion on us; you will tread our sins underfoot and hurl all our iniquities into the depths of the sea" (Micah 7:19; see Psalm 103).

If there are reparations to be made, of course, make them. But see the slate as wiped clean—and, if you can, laugh at any silliness. Take a deep breath and walk on. Ask once again for His guidance. Any unpleasant feelings remaining will fade away. And step by step, day by day, year by year, you will learn to hear His voice more consistently. Just give Him—and yourself—time.

You would think I would know better by now (especially after you read my note to women in chapter 10), but I missed the boat once again just recently. Our son Tom was about to receive an MBA and his office wanted to surprise him with a computerized slide "roast" to celebrate. One of his associates e-mailed me, asking if I could scan and send a few pictures showing Tom at various ages.

Bill watched me e-mail off a few and finally said, "Where is one from his Army days?"

"Oh, I don't think"—that *I think* should have made me pause right there and listen some more, but I breezed on—"they would care about that. Besides, I can only send three or four, and I have such cute ones already!"

"I still feel you should send one," Bill said.

I ignored him, which for me, because long ago I made a pact to hear the Lord through Bill, is tantamount to ignoring God.

Sure enough, the next morning I found an e-mail raving about the selections I had sent, and then adding, "But I don't see any here from his military service, and I know we'd like one of those, especially with his hair cut short!"

Laughing, I scanned in a photo Bill held ready in his hand, and asked his and the Lord's forgiveness.

It may seem a small thing, but it helps me learn big lessons.

Once Over Lightly

Learning to discern is just that: learning. And all learning involves failure along the way. But for us who belong to the Lord, failure does not lead to hell. It leads us over and over to the loving heart of God. It shows us the depth of the sea of forgiveness and grace. All of it we will ever need is there, and more.

When you fall, don't hide; confess and receive forgiveness. Keep short accounts, and give God time to renew you.

Failing and falling? More space for grace!

Now let's look at some of the special ways the Lord speaks to us.

Your Turn to Discern

1. Where have you failed to discern the Lord?

2. Was it because you missed Him? Or did not try to hear Him?

3. Have you ever acted like Jonah, hearing and deciding not to obey?

4. Each time you fail, have you asked forgiveness? If not, it is never too late. Clean out the tubes and keep short accounts!

5. How can you tell the difference between the Lord's conviction of sin and the enemy's hassling? Can you think of some examples from your own life?

6. As you grow in the Lord, can you see how you are maturing in discerning His voice? If you cannot see it, ask Him about it.

eight

Nudges and Knowings

Nudges and knowings are two of the wonderful ways God communicates with us.

Nudges jog our memories or thoughts to move us to appropriate action. Most often nudges are a fun part of life with the Lord. They are His interventions in our everyday routines. They show the helpful, practical, personal side of the Almighty, and are based on premises we have already discussed: We want to hear from God. He wants us to hear from Him. He knows He will usually have to act first to get our attention in our busy, fragmented lives and minds.

Hey, the nudge says. *Look at that person or situation. Invite Me into it; set Me free. Pray or act—whatever you hear Me saying.*

Knowings, as I call them, are the dreams or images of things to come we know deep down, at a gut level, to be from the Lord. They can comfort us when we are hurt or bewildered, or excite our curiosity and hope when we are in the doldrums. They can keep us going in a dark time.

When a knowing involves something that is yet to happen, there is nothing we have to do to make this event occur. It is in the hands of God.

Nudges: Bumps in Our Thinking

"In order to be a better husband, a man should. . . ."
The speaker's words caught my wandering attention.
Aha! I thought. *Bill needs to hear this part.*

I raised an elbow and gave his rib cage a jab. He jumped a bit and grinned at me. My nudge had worked, at least in getting his attention.

The American Heritage Dictionary of the English Language defines *nudge* as "to push against gently, esp. to gain attention or give a signal." Human beings nudge one another often. Parents may touch a child's shoulder or tap the seat of his pants. This is to get his attention and encourage him to obey or to do something, preferably right now.

Teachers and professors nudge us verbally. We stand in class, sweaty-palmed, trying to express an idea we only half-understand.

Miss Block says, "Yes, Roberta? Yes! That's right, *and . . .* ?"
Her nudge encourages me to fill in the blanks in my thinking. It pushes me along in my knowledge.

When God gives nudges, they are not usually felt as a physical jab or tap, but they *are* sudden bumps in our thinking that startle us to attention and move us along in our faith. His nudge may come as an unexpected, interjected reference to a person or event in our welter of thoughts. Or it may come as the sudden realization that we are mulling over an event or a name or the image of a person. This can happen once, or over many minutes, or over many days.

"Huh? Oh—yes, Lord?" This is the reaction God is after. He wants me to stop rambling around in these thoughts and listen for what He wants me to do with them. Most of the time He wants me to focus my thinking and intercede for that person or event. Usually I never know the reason or results, but I learn to hear and obey God and let go of my need to understand.

Sometimes, however, I do find out why I was nudged. Our youngest son, David, was born on a cold January morning. By three that afternoon a blizzard raged outside the hospital. As I inched myself down under the covers to take a well-deserved nap, I suddenly found myself thinking about Jan and Jill Cady, twin daughters of my friend Betty. As teens the twins had often babysat for us.

I yawned and prayed something like, *God, Jan and Jill are suddenly in my mind. Please bless them. Be with them. If there is some need, thank You for taking care of it.*

Then I fell asleep.

A few days later Betty called me to rejoice in David's birth.

"I won't forget his birthday!" Betty said. "Jan and Jill had quite an experience in that storm. They were on I-70 near Columbus when they hit an icy patch. They slid out of control across four lanes of interstate and wound up headed the wrong way just off the pavement. Motorists stopped and helped them get turned around and on their way. Everyone said it was a miracle that their car didn't hit anyone else's as it skidded across all those lanes. They came home shaking and crying, but praising God."

"What time did that happen?" I asked, with more than a little curiosity.

"Oh, let me think." Betty paused. "Well, they got in about four, so it must have happened right around three o'clock. . . ."

Would God have saved Jan and Jill if I had ignored the nudge and not bothered to pray? Of course. If He really needed a prayer to act, He would have nudged someone until He got the prayer He needed. But because I accepted the sudden appearance of their names in my mind as a reminder to pray, I had the joy of being part of God's plan—and, in this case, learning why as well.

Sometimes a nudge comes as a memory that surfaces suddenly, like the shrapnel from war days that we talked about earlier. It may be something that hurts or embarrasses me to think about. God was there even if I did not know it, and the memory has now appeared for me to look at without fear, inside His love. I may need to ask and receive forgiveness for my part in it. Or I may need to give unasked-for forgiveness to another person and pray for him or her.

THREE PURPOSES

Nudges serve at least three wonderful purposes in growing me up in the Lord:

They enable me to practice discerning His voice in my thoughts.

They give me ways to practice being obedient to what I perceive His will or plan to be.

They encourage me to reach beyond my own problems to intercede for others.

The first time I ever thought of God nudging me was when a pastor interrupted a discussion we were having in his study. An emergency squad had just careened by outside, siren blaring.

"Let me stop a second," he said. "I always use the sound of sirens as a signal to pray for whoever is in trouble."

I began practicing that, too.

Later I let God program me to block out the endless hours of my journalist-husband's radio scanner except when the calls with "10–50, P.I." ("Vehicle accident with personal injury") or "Subject not breathing" came on. Sometimes, as I follow the action on the police channels, I have sensed that my prayers, no doubt coupled with those of others equally unknown, have helped bring about terse updated reports: "10–50 is a P.D. [property damage] only" or "Subject is now breathing." Occasionally I have read accounts later of those accidents in the papers, with the police quoted as saying, "It was a miracle this person survived."

Sometimes the nudge is not to pray but to act. It does not have to be some dramatic action, such as two I will share later in this section. I learned early in my new faith life, as part of practicing the presence of God, to invite Him to shop with me. Some people feel it is silly to ask God to be part of the daily trivia of life, but as a young mother, trivia was all I had. Over the years, asking the Lord to participate in the minutia of my life has been fun and miraculous, and it has become a way of life for me. But it is still a never-ending learning process.

Recently, on the way to the grocery store, I asked the Lord to help me remember what I needed and to help me buy wisely within my budget. When I reached the toothpaste and medicine aisle, I found my hand reaching for a box of ibuprofen. I was down to two tablets in the bottle at home.

No, I thought, *I don't need this.*

The picture of a new box in the linen closet, sticking out of a jumble of Band-Aids, zinc tablets and furniture polish rose in my mind. I put the ibuprofen back on the shelf, argued with one more tiny nudge in the name of "sensible buying habits" and moved on.

That evening I went to replace the bottle in the bathroom. There in the linen closet I did find a new box. Of aspirin.

O Lord! I sighed ruefully. *That was You, helping me out in the little things, just as I asked. Please forgive me again.*

Being a gracious Lord and Father, He gave me another chance three days later to listen, hear and obey.

Some months earlier my friend Linda Smith had treated me to a birthday lunch at the mall, and as part of it bought me a huge plastic mug. On subsequent visits to the eatery, this could be refilled for a fraction of the usual price. Unfortunately I seldom remembered to take it with me.

On that Monday I was out of the house and starting the car when the thought struck: *Maybe you'd best get lunch before hitting the grocery. And go back for that mug!*

Oh, I don't need it, I thought. Then I recalled arguing with the supermarket nudge about ibuprofen. *Better to err on the side of obedience.*

I sighed, unstrapped the seatbelt, ran back into the house and grabbed the mug off the kitchen shelf.

At the mall half an hour later, I ordered the mug filled with iced tea. Suddenly I heard a familiar voice behind me. "Hi, Bobbi!"

It was Linda. We had not seen each other since that birthday treat. Yet because I had obeyed this nudge, the timing was perfect for the unexpected joy of another lunch with her. And I even had her birthday mug with me.

Amid the turmoil on this planet, the wars and rumors of war, the famines and lawlessness and loneliness, this small personal kindness from God to one woman may strike you as ridiculously unimportant. But God cares. He can oversee the whole universe and still be involved intimately in the details of an individual life. His nudges are a constant reminder of this. They are always special, specific, to me, to you. In His nudges I see Him as an ever-present, caring Father in ways that, without them, I might not.

CHECKING YOUR NUDGES

So how do I know if a sudden thought is one of God's nudges? Well, I can quickly run some of the pocket tests on it, if necessary, that we looked at in chapter 6. As in the case of the supermarket situation, however, one of my best tests is if I suddenly find myself arguing with the idea: *No, I don't think I need this item. . . . I don't think it's really practical. . . .*

With whom am I arguing? If it is my idea, I would not be arguing with myself about it, would I? And if it is a nudge to pray, it isn't a "plant" from an unholy spirit. Satan would never want me to pray, believing. So usually I realize I am arguing with God. If the nudge passes the Scripture and loving tests, then I can act on it.

I have learned that it is always O.K. to err on the side of obedience. It is my heart, after all, that God sees. As long as we both know that I want to hear and obey, then I cannot lose if I practice obedience. He can turn my mistakes into blessings. Remember Tib Sherrill's guests with the prayers about the peas? Although perhaps they should have asked God about the timing or discomfiting method of their discerning, I know God was infinitely pleased with the desire in those two hearts to seek His will in all things. And now their learning process helps teach *us* decades later!

If your nudge involves actively doing something for or with (or saying something to) someone else, then you need to be very sure not only that you have heard the Lord's will, but that you know what His timing and method are. Not only the *what* but the *when* and *how* have to be God's, as you recall. If you ask, He will let you know.

If the timing for when you act on the nudge is a concern, then you can also discern whether you are feeling rushed and pushed. If you are feeling hassled, confused or shoved against your will to do this thing *right now*, it may or may not be the Lord who is nudging you. If you feel that you *must* do this thing, again, it may or may not be the Lord. Stop and pray and apply a few more tests to the nudge.

If you feel serenely moved along in doing this, however, then most probably it *is* the Lord. His peace, even in urgent situations, is unmistakable. Again, it is your heart God wants and sees. If you are in doubt, it is O.K. to err on the side of obedience. Also, He does not mind if you ask Him several times! (Remember Gideon?)

I have received most of my nudges from God within the context of my daily wife-and-mother life. This is the very place the Lord wants to remind me how real and present He is. Whether His nudges have been soft or hard, I cannot think of a single time I was sorry I obeyed one—and I can think of several times when I was genuinely sorry I did not. When I know I have missed Him, I have learned not to hide behind an excuse. I ask His forgiveness, accept it and move on. (Remember what we covered in the previous chapter?)

Even when I never see any reason for why I prayed or did something, I always feel good that at least I tried to hear and obey God—and I know He is pleased.

Listening for the Shepherd's voice, choosing to obey Him, finding Him in everyday life, learning to ask and seek forgiveness quickly when I fail. . . . Nudges give me the opportunity to practice all these.

NUDGES WITH TEETH

God has more active nudges, too. These are times when God's power more than nudges—it shoves!

OBEDIENCE ON TURKEY HILL ROAD

Nancy Hutchinson and I had finished our weekly prayer time. Heading home, she drove south on narrow, twisting Turkey Hill Road, steering absentmindedly around the first curves above the creek and continuing down into the brief level stretch.

Suddenly an almost-audible voice filled the car. *Slow down!*

Startled, Nancy glanced over her shoulder but saw nothing. Nonetheless she let up on the accelerator. The car slowed from 35 to 25.

I said, Slow down!

This time the presence of a voice was so strong that Nancy said involuntarily, "Yes, sir!" and took her foot entirely off the accelerator. Her sedan coasted into the bottom of the next uphill curve at about ten miles an hour.

Just then a car full of teens careened down the curve, completely in Nancy's lane. For a split second their frightened faces stared into Nancy's. Then their car swerved back toward the other side, missing her by inches, and roared away.

Shaking, Nancy poured out her thanks to God as she accelerated and drove on.

Could Nancy have chosen to disobey this voice? Probably, although it is doubtful that she would have. With a nudge like this, God's peace and the power to obey seem to come with it.

BILL IN THE AIRPLANE

Sometimes God nudges us even before we know it is He.

During the first year after the Lord walked into my life, Bill was amused and bemused by the changes he saw in his wife. For the most part he was glad for me but disinterested for himself.

Rationalism and agnosticism suited the journalist in him just fine—until the October night he lost the engine on the single-engine plane he was piloting over the dark fields of central Ohio.

He and my brother had flown from Newark, Ohio, to Delaware, Ohio. It was dusk as they took off and headed east toward Newark again. Suddenly there was a loud *bang!* in the engine. The plane began to vibrate. Bill called the control tower at Port Columbus Airport, twenty miles south. He wanted desperately to try to get home, but the approach to Newark Airport was over housing subdivisions. He chose to turn back toward the more rural strip.

"Roger," the controller said. "We will vector you to Delaware."

By the time they were rattling and banging in the area of Delaware Airport, it was fully dark and the runway was no longer visible. The men in the windowless room in the Columbus control tower had forgotten that Daylight Savings Time had ended the day before. Once they remembered and informed Bill how to turn on the runway lights with his microphone button, the little plane was directly over the runway and much too high to land.

"I'm going out to make another approach," Bill radioed as he swung the shaking plane south to circle back.

As he started banking gently southeast, the rattling and banging suddenly stopped. The engine had died.

Concentrating on the sinking plane, Bill tossed the microphone to my brother, who radioed, "We've lost our engine! We're going down!"

A quarter of a mile away, Bill could see the runway, now clearly lit. It was temptingly close. But without power could they make the final turns? Most likely they would not reach the safety of the airstrip before running out of altitude or airspeed. But what was his alternative?

Go straight ahead.

A strong voice spoke just over his shoulder. Full of peace and authority, it reminded him of the voices of his respected senior Marine officers. Should he obey it? A glance at my brother's face showed he had heard no voice. To go straight meant flying across the runway, out into the dark, trying to hold the plane level until it hit the ground, trusting it would not strike an obstacle or flip over. Bill hesitated.

Go straight ahead.

The voice was softer but still firm. Bill squared his shoulders. He knew Authority when he heard it.

"I'm going to land straight ahead," he said.

My brother nodded.

Into the dark they flew. Seconds ticked by like hours as the aircraft dropped. Then *bump, bump, bump,* the plane was down, right side up, unscathed. The two men sat and breathed for a moment. Then, as the gyros whined down, they popped open the door of the plane and started their hike back to the airport.

Daylight showed that they had glided in over a hedgerow between two trees and stopped in a freshly plowed soybean field, just short of power lines and railroad tracks. It was the only place around where they could have slid in without turning over.

The FAA investigator told me later, based on his many experiences with incidents of this kind, that if Bill had tried for the runway, they almost certainly would have been killed.

Bill did not tell me about the Voice until years afterward, but from that night on his own faith began to come alive.

Could he have disobeyed this Voice? Certainly—but again, an audible shove came with the power to believe and obey implicitly, as my husband sensed that this Voice knew the truth. Even a rationalist and agnostic recognized it!

These are exciting nudges—strong, direct interventions of God that save lives.

Knowings: Special Gifts of Faith

Knowings, as I call them, are different from nudges. Some people may actually experience revelations or dreams or visions. But those scriptural events often involve some action to be taken. For me a knowing is an inner picture or idea that I do not have to act on, but that has a strong, peaceful sense of absolute truth at the core of it. I know this "something," whatever it is, at an intuitive level.

Unlike a nudge, about which I have to do something, I simply ponder a knowing in my heart until it happens.

One of the earliest knowings I remember was during the winter of my senior year in college, before I really knew the Lord, but not before He knew me. I had met Bill Rogers, an alumnus who had graduated six years ahead of me, more than a year before and we had dated each other, among others, for fifteen months. My heart sensed he was far more special than any of my other dates. But suddenly he stopped calling or coming around. We had not had an argument; he just dropped out of my life.

Every weekend I hung around near the dorm phone in case he called. I was hurt and angry and bewildered. And the real reason was, way down underneath it all, I *knew* he could not be gone for good. I knew he was supposed to be a permanent part of my life. Beneath my emotions lay a strong knowing that I could not acknowledge at a conscious level.

When Bill started calling again a few months later (with no explanation of why he had stopped!), the surface level of me was delighted and relieved. The deepest part of me said, *Of course. This is the way it was meant to be.*

A knowing is like a special gift of faith. I do not get them very often and have not grown far enough in my faith life, even after 25 years, to act on them or always stand up in the face of doubt and say absolutely, "I *know* God has said this!" (We will deal with doubt in the next chapter.)

It is me I distrust. *Am I really hearing God?* I ask myself. But at least now I can let the knowing lie there in my life and wait. And more and more I can let it do what I think God wants most for it to do: comfort me in bewildering times.

KNOWING GOD AS ABBA

For many years after that April day when the Lord came to me, I knew Christians who talked about God as their Father in a way that I did not experience. They seemed to have a close, intimate *Abba* (Daddy) relationship with Him, much as Jesus had (see Mark 14:36; Romans 8:15; Galatians 4:6). I understood this relationship with my head. I longed for it with my heart. But I did not possess it. Like a dusty cobweb, the question hung in the corners of my life for years: *Why can't I sense, know, love and feel love from God as my Abba?*

Rationally I knew that part of the reason lay in the tangled, broken relationship I had with my earthly father. Yet over the years I had truly forgiven Dad and moved on, accepting the childhood I did and did not have as something God would now work for good. Yet I could never seem to feel God's presence as an intimate Abba.

Then, about eighteen years into my faith life, my earthly father developed terminal cancer. As I dealt with his dying, I got a knowing deep inside me one day. It came, as they often do, as a piece of a concept, a flash of an idea.

When your earthly father is gone, then I will reveal Myself to you as Abba.

Just as fast, I heard myself wonder, *Why only then? I've never had a close relationship with Dad. Why would God have to wait until after his death?*

Instantaneously I had another thought, one that could not have come from my selfish thinking.

Because in spite of his fierce anger and strict façade, your father has always been a very insecure person. I, God, would never usurp what little father-daughter love the two of you have. He is too fragile about himself to understand about My being your Father. And you need to have all your daddy love, however little, directed toward the man I appointed as your earthly father for as long as he is alive.

There was no condemnation in this exchange of ideas. It came and went in a second or two. There was nothing for me to do but to tuck this idea up in my heart and wait and see if it happened.

It did. A few months after Dad died—our reconciliation at his deathbed as complete as it could be—I began to notice a new element in my nightly prayers. I found myself talking to God as if I were a very little girl, then snuggling down under the blankets as if I were being tucked in. I would stretch out a hand "for my daddy to hold" in the dark night—and I was not envisioning an earthly father. Slowly that knowing became a reality. The great, omnipotent Creator God became my Abba—my first, real, there-for-me Daddy.

Several things confirmed that knowing as being the Lord's voice. First, there was no condemnation about my past relationship with either the Lord or my earthly father. Second, the revelation about my father was so full of agape love that it could not have come from me. I honestly had not known or cared whether my father's persona was fragile or not. From my viewpoint all the hurt was mine. And third, with no effort on my part, the event pictured in the knowing happened. After my earthly father's death, God at last became my Abba.

DEALING WITH DIFFICULT KNOWINGS

This is often the way with what I call knowings. The words or mental pictures or phrase-thoughts come—maybe out of the blue, maybe triggered by a Scripture. You receive them. You ponder them from time to time in your heart. Maybe you pray about them wistfully or wishfully. And then God fulfills them.

If you experience any ongoing terror or dread connected to something you know is going to happen, it is not the Holy Spirit bringing this to you. (Remember the tests we run to see if an idea is from the Lord or not? *No fear!* is one of the prime ones.)

When I was in my young twenties, a friend professed to me that she knew deep inside that she would not have a long life. She sensed she would die young, probably before she was forty. Her shared secret troubled me, and I sensed that she was saddened, even frightened, knowing this thing about herself. Now that we are both well into our sixth decades, I see it was not a God-given knowing. The fruit was fear, vague dread and niggling worry. The event did not occur. It was not a knowing from God.

On the other hand, God once had a wise old man tell a very young woman something awful: "This child is destined to cause the falling and rising of many in Israel, and to be a sign that will be spoken against, so that the thoughts of many hearts will be revealed. And a sword will pierce your own soul too" (Luke 2:34–35).

I often wonder how Mary dealt with those unsettling words of Simeon's over the next 33 years. My guess, based on a few other Scriptures about her, is that she pondered them in her heart. That is what she did with words spoken about and by Jesus in the first two chapters of Luke. And because Simeon's revelation was indeed God's word—a knowing from Him—I would guess that the peace that passes understanding surrounded those difficult words whenever Mary pondered them. I do not believe she lived in dread of whatever that terrible sword meant, but dealt with her thoughts about it in a detached, trusting way: "Well, Lord, whatever it is, I know You'll handle it."

At the cross, when her heart must have broken as they pierced her son, I believe hope still sang deep in her soul. The reason I think so is this: Mary did not fade away in her grief. Instead, as we read in Acts 2, she waited expectantly, along with the disciples, for that Pentecost outpouring. She, too, was filled with the Holy Spirit that morning. She found the fulfillment of joy in knowing that her Jesus was the One who now threw open the gates of heaven and life eternal to whoever would receive them. The difficult knowing had come and gone. The sword had pierced but not destroyed.

Once Over Lightly

Nudges almost always require some action. Knowings do not. A nudge often urges you to pray, but sometimes it requires you to act, and fairly quickly. If you feel steadily pushed, or strongly and serenely moved along to action (as Nancy and Bill were), it is most likely the Lord. If you have already asked the Lord to be part of whatever you are doing (such as I had at the supermarket) and you find yourself arguing with a nudge, that is a clue to stop and err on the side of obeying it! The important thing to the Lord is that your heart wants to hear and obey Him, not that you always get it right. You have the freedom to fail and to ask God to make it right.

Knowings, as I call them, are strong ideas that form inside you, but, unlike nudges, you do not have to act on them. They will always be scriptural in nature but not necessarily in so many words. They will never involve the things God hates or forbids. Knowings spring from a quick inner conversation or from some overview—a vision, perhaps, or a prophecy or dream about an event. They are accompanied by deep peace, an ability to simply receive them and occasionally wonder about them, but as a disinterested spectator.

There is usually nothing you have to do to make that knowing happen. If it is from the Lord, then He will accomplish it. You will experience a peaceful detachment. God is in control and He is doing it all.

Knowings are for the long run. At heart you can trust them. Whether you choose to believe a knowing or not, there is no condemnation. It is God's job to fulfill it, and yours simply to wait. Waiting with faith will give you peace. "Let the peace of Christ rule in your [heart]" (Colossians 3:15). The peace that far surpasses our understanding is the bottom line in everything told us by God.

Nudges give us some of the most basic, day-to-day ways to hear God's voice. They give us practice in listening, testing and then obeying. They bring the already-there reality of God into the details of our lives as nothing else can.

141

Nudges and knowings are special ways we hear our
Shepherd's voice. But they often come with large
spaces where doubt can climb in and nibble at us.
So how do we deal with doubt and other ugly
things?

Your Turn to Discern

1. Sirens and police scanners are two of the places that
serve as permanent prayer nudges for me. Where does
God give you regular nudges to pray?

2. Can you think of other nudges you have experienced recently? How did you react to them?

3. When you realized you might have misheard God,
did you hide? Or did you admit your error and receive
His loving forgiveness? If an example springs to mind,
confess to Him now.

4. Has God ever given you a knowing? How did you
react to it while you were waiting for it to come? Did it
give you a sense of hope or comfort during a difficult
time?

5. Do you have a knowing now? What is it telling
you? Have you tested its fruit to see if it is the Lord?

Doubts, Fears and Other Horrible Things

When we seek to discern the Lord's will—His voice—for us, we soon find ourselves face to face with a gaggle of unpleasant emotions or circumstances. We find doubt, fear, worry, vague guilt and situations we do not understand hissing and honking at us like angry geese. God knows they are there; it is our job to recognize them, too, and get busy shooing them away.

The Lord does not speak to us through doubt, fear, worry or vague guilt. If you are listening to any of these ugly things, you are not hearing the Lord. But He can use all these to help us grow in faith and discernment.

Doubt: The Very First Temptation

"Did God *really* say . . . ?" the snake hissed into Eve's ear.

She may have tried to refute the idea that God was withholding something good from her and Adam, but the doubt was planted. She began to entertain the thought. She saw with her eyes how innocent and luscious the fruit looked. *Hmmm, maybe the snake was right. . . .*

She sampled the forbidden fruit and took it to Adam. Neither sought to discern the truth from God Himself. So Eve's doubt gave birth to disbelief, and disbelief to disobedience—for Adam and Eve and for all of us since. Eve did not practice discernment in her weak moment, and it cost all of us Eden.

Doubt follows us around and nibbles at the edges of our faith. It asks us questions we cannot answer. It whispers ugly things in our ears. It causes us to stumble. Sometimes it becomes so loud in our thoughts that we choose to believe the doubt instead of the truth. Doubt is often fueled by the fires of hell and borne to us on the mutters of invisible ungodly beings.

Hannah Whitall Smith, writing a century ago in *Everyday Religion*, was specific about this: "Doubts and uncertainties about spiritual things belong to and come from the ungodly spirit of this world."

Some believe doubt is *"the* sin that so easily entangles" (Hebrews 12:1, emphasis added), and that it is because of the great cloud of faith-fulfilled witnesses that we can shrug it off and keep going.

Even so, doubt is permitted by God, so we have to face it and deal with it, one doubt at a time. The lovely irony is that as we tackle our doubts and choose to believe in the face of them, our faith grows stronger. No wonder God has left those niggling little things here to try us; they lose, we win!

Sometimes, however, as I try to discern something, I begin to wonder if I fit into James 1:5–8. (By the way, to wonder *if* can be the first sign of an impending doubt!)

> If any of you lacks wisdom, he should ask God, who gives generously to all without finding fault, and it will be given to him. But when he asks, he must believe and not doubt, because he who doubts is like a wave of the sea, blown and tossed by

the wind. That man should not think he will receive anything from the Lord; he is a double-minded man, unstable in all he does.

James 1:5–8

Perhaps you have experienced this, too. Let's say you or your spouse receives a new job offer. It may cause some financial disruption and a move at first, but the future prospects are much better than the current job. You have prayed and believe this is the direction God wants. But after you have begun to pack the dishes, an argument begins to nibble at you.

"Do I really believe and not doubt that God wants us to do this?"

No. I do doubt sometimes.

"So am I one of those double-minded people, unstable in all I do?"

Gee, I'm not sure; I hope not.

"Have I really heard the Lord at all?"

Gosh, maybe I blew it. Maybe we shouldn't make this move.

Suddenly you are plunged into gloom, being "blown and tossed by the wind." You are caught up in doubt.

Doubt comes from the Latin *dubitare*, "to waver." It includes the concepts "to be undecided or skeptical; to tend to disbelieve; distrust"; and it engenders "a lack of conviction or certainty." If I use only the Latin root with a dictionary definition of *doubt*, you and I often fit neatly into the Scripture above.

Oh, dear! How are we ever going to be sure we heard the Lord?

But while we have one word translated *doubt*, the Greeks had six verbs and one noun for the concept. In Greek the verb *to doubt* can mean "to be perplexed," "to be perplexed to the point of despair," "to be uncertain with small faith," "to be anxious or distracted," "to be in suspense due to failure of expectations" and "to waver with lack of faith." The Greek word James used in the passage above, according to *Vine's Expository Dictionary of Old and New Testament Words*, was *diakrino*, the final meaning in that list, implying "not so much weakness of faith, as lack of it."

If you and I are the Lord's, His pilgrims along the Way, then we are *not* among the doubters to whom James refers. Our faith may seem weak at moments, but it is definitely alive and growing. We are not the "doubleminded" ones—which in Greek is *dipsuchos* or "two-souled"—who will receive nothing from the Lord. We are singlehearted followers of Jesus Christ.

We can learn much from this Scripture, but we need not be thrown into doubt and despair that we are wavering. This verse is warning skeptics, not believers. You can push ahead with packing your dishes, then, in faith that if the Lord is not in this, He will close the door. You can "doubt not."

DOUBTING DOUBT

In the scientific world doubt has many practical uses. Look at all the theories about fat in the diet. Someone proposed a theory, another researcher doubted it and proved the opposite, another questioned that and found a third possibility. This is healthy doubt, since man's ideas may or may not be true.

As Christians, however, we come up against an interesting paradox about doubt. When applied to Scripture, if there is something to *doubt*, then there is obviously the opposite—something to *believe*. Because Christians have access to the truth, any doubt that sets itself up in opposition to that truth is a lie.

Does this mean we should simply reject all anti-Scriptural doubts and move on without paying them any attention? As we grow in faith and in the knowledge of the Lord, we might find that this is exactly what we *will* do. But in the meantime our doubts can become useful tools to help us get closer to the Lord. They force us to seek His help. And He will help us.

In my early months as a Christian, I sometimes found myself doubting that God existed at all, and that anything that had happened to me since that April afternoon was real. (Like most doubts, this one sounds startlingly like the snake's hiss to Eve: "Did God really . . . ?") I wondered if I had just made it all up and convinced myself of its truth. But by God's grace, I had the reminder of my uncallused thumbs.

I was born with calluses on the front pads of my thumbs. "She was busy sucking her thumb in there!" the obstetrician told my mother. I soon became busy sucking my thumb out here, too. In fact, no matter what my parents tried over the years, nothing worked. I chewed through gloves and put up with applications of bitter liquids. I was impervious to both positive and negative reinforcement.

To my horror, I grew into womanhood unable to stop sucking my thumb. It was the most humiliating thing I could think of about myself. I hid it from college roommates, and was able to sneak into the ladies' room when I taught school, but shortly before we married I had to tell Bill that he might wake up and find me inadvertently sucking my thumb. Not one night in my life had I been able to fall asleep without my thumb. Never had I been able to relax from a tense time without it. Whenever I thought well of myself, I remembered my dark little problem and was filled with shame.

I sucked my thumb every day and night for 31 years, until a few weeks after the Lord walked into my life. Suddenly, like an alcoholic miraculously released from all desire and need to drink, I fell asleep one night in June without my thumb in my mouth.

After several nights like this, I realized what was happening. I was so incredulous that I ran a test. Before I went to bed one night, I put on bright red lipstick. If I sucked my thumb in my sleep, it would be ringed with red at the base the next morning.

I awoke in the pre-dawn dark, ran to the bathroom and flipped on the light. There was no trace of red on either thumb. God had just given me something to help me laugh at my doubts as a young Christian. The hissing doubts were lying; God was real, and so was what had happened to me.

As I grew older in the Lord, those initial doubts stopped assailing me; new ones took—and take—their place. But it is ever easier to see them for exactly what they are: *doubts*. And doubts about anything revealed in Scripture lie. More and more I laugh at them, knowing that the opposite of what they suggest is the truth. Their very presence, trying to get me to disbelieve, often confirms my faith in something I have discerned and gives me greater confidence in it.

Again, Hannah Whitall Smith was unequivocal about doubting anything the Lord has told us in Scripture. In *The Christian's Secret of a Happy Life* she wrote: "To have doubts arise is not sinful. But . . . it is always sinful to indulge doubts. . . . Doubts and discouragements are always from an evil source and are always untrue."

How about you? If you analyze the doubts you have faced in your journey of faith, you, too, will probably see how they lied and how God's loving presence enabled you to grow through them.

IF YOU DOUBT, CHECK IT OUT!

Doubt can be harder to refute when we are trying to discern whether an idea or thought is especially from the Lord for us. There is something in us that has a hard time believing God wants to and does talk to us, or that, if He does, we can hear Him correctly. It is the *timing* of a doubt that can help us determine what to do with it.

BEFORE DISCERNMENT: "IF YOU DOUBT, DON'T"

Before reaching a decision, I have found that a particular rule usually works: *If you doubt, don't.* While I am still in the process of testing an idea, I do not act on it until the Lord's peace comes. That doubt needs to be added to my discernment tests. I might pray, "Lord, I am doubting this. Please reveal the truth to me." Then I wait some more.

AFTER DISCERNMENT: "IF YOU DOUBT, PRAY AND KEEP GOING"

Once I have tested an idea and believe that an action or attitude and its timing are His for me, then another premise usually applies: *If you doubt, pray and forge ahead.* Now doubt is most likely the enemy, setting up roadblocks. I keep on toward the goal set for me and pray about the doubt. Maybe I even rebuke it. Or I say, "Lord, I discerned that this is what You want me to do. I have this doubt and am pretty sure it isn't from You. If it is, if I have misheard You, then feel free to enable me to hear You. Otherwise I'm going to keep doing what I have tested and believe You want."

Dale Becraft uses the "open door" test for doubts. "If I believe God has asked me to do something," he says, "then when doubt creeps in, I simply ask God to keep the door that is from Him open and close the rest. Then I keep walking until I hit a closed door. Instead of trying to kick that open, I stop and reassess things with God."

Our goal is to hear and obey God. When we doubt, He is delighted to deliver us. Remember the first part of the James passage on not doubting? This is what we, heirs of the King, can learn from it: He is a God "who gives generously to all without finding fault," and if we lack wisdom, we should "ask God, . . . and it will be given to [us]" (James 1:5).

So don't be afraid when doubt assails you. Talk it over with the God who gives generously and who will do so without finding fault. He will not be mad at you for doubting, especially if you are honest about it. Remember His grace!

In the world you will want to check out your doubts. But in the Kingdom of God, any doubt as to the revealed nature and truth of God can be disregarded instantly. God does not speak through doubt.

"Did God *really* say you will hear His voice?" the snake may hiss.

"Absolutely!" you can respond joyfully.

And if you listen carefully, you can hear joyous laughter echoing in heaven. Doubt must flee. The snake slithers away. Faith has won.

"CHECKS IN MY SPIRIT"

Have you ever heard someone say, regarding a situation or course of action, "I have a check in my spirit about that"? It comes with an "Mmmm, I don't know about this. . . ." in that person's tone.

A "check" is the first cousin of a doubt. It is there to offer a momentary pause in our discernment process.

A check *in* someone's spirit may or may not be a check *by* the Holy Spirit. We must discern whether it is the person's spirit or the Holy One asking us to pray and think some more before we act. The other person's check, or our own, may be a red flag waving; or a yellow, cautionary one; or just a smoke-screen from the enemy.

The first-century disciples sought to hear the Lord after His resurrection and ascension, just as we do. And they were bold to report their conclusions. Peter told His fellow believers about the three men sent by Cornelius: "The Spirit told me to have no hesitation about going with them" (Acts 11:12). Luke wrote in Acts 16:6–7: "Paul and his companions . . . [were] kept by the Holy Spirit from preaching the word in the province of Asia. . . . They tried to enter Bithynia, but the Spirit of Jesus would not allow them to."

The apostles had both "go aheads" and "checks" in the Spirit, all right! God told them in an inner voice (and sometimes an audible one—remember Saul on the Damascus road) that they clearly recognized as that of Jesus. Much as you might hear your father's or mother's voice deep in your heart as you face choices he or she tried to teach you how to make as a child, so the disciples and Paul had seen and heard Jesus up close and personal. They knew something we cannot: the actual sound of His voice.

Yet the same Spirit who spoke into their thoughts and hearts is available to us. He wants us to hear Him just as much as He did the disciples. But we have an advantage: We have the Scripture in easily available form to look at again and again as a test for His voice, even though we have no personal knowledge of what Jesus' earthly voice sounded like. If someone says to you about something, "I have a check in my spirit," check out the check. It may or may not be the Lord whispering in your heart.

LISTENING FOR LANGUAGE

In spiritual matters, certain phrases I hear coming from my own mouth, or from that of another Christian, become checks or warning flags indicating that I need to stop and listen for the Lord more carefully. Each statement starts with the big *I*:

"I think. . . ."

"I believe. . . ."

"I know. . . ."

Each one of these phrases may suggest a different meaning.

The phrase *I think* (and its cousin, *I feel*) can sometimes reveal just what it says: that the person is doing the thinking here. It is the human mind that thinks something is true or not, and, as we have seen, human thoughts may or may not contain truth. If someone says, "I think the Lord wants . . .", you would be wise to hear the *I think* part before you act on the *the Lord wants* part, testing the idea with Scripture and the ever-ready Holy Spirit.

At the same time it is good to remember, as a friend wrote me, "I always want to allow for the possibility that I'm wrong, and avoid being a steamroller. The phrase *I think* can also communicate modesty or humility and a desire not to be overly dogmatic or forceful."

The phrase *I believe* may show a bit more conviction on the part of the speaker. When you hear it from someone, listen carefully and test the thoughts scripturally. This person may be onto what the Lord wants. The phrase *I believe* is also a wonderful, loving way to share something you know is true without sounding dogmatic. For example: "Honey, I believe we really need to make this decision now, not next week."

The phrase *I know* usually contains great conviction. The implication: "I am certain this is from the Lord." If the speaker is a maturing Christian, you can go boldly before the Lord and say, "Father, the idea to do [whatever] comes strongly from So-and-So, whose judgment I trust. I believe it is probably You. If I am wrong, then please correct me." Once again, it is our willing, obedient hearts God is after, not perfection.

So listen to the phrases coming from your own mouth and from others. Let "I think, I believe, I know" represent cautions for you in hearing the Lord's heart. Spend a bit more time praying and reading Scripture before you act.

Fear: It Always Lies

I am one of the world's experts on fear! The central lesson of my own life with the Lord so far has been learning how to live without it. I picked up the scriptural premises early, but actually living in the secure confidence the Lord intends for His children has taken 25 years (and still counting) of practice. But I *am* learning.

In learning to discern, if you are struck by fear as you seek to hear the Lord, or if a thought or idea comes to you with fear hanging on its apron strings, or if you are afraid to do or *not* do something, remember that fear is no indicator of truth. The reason for this I learned well: *Fear lies.*

Except for the adrenaline-rush reaction that God gives us to flee real and present danger, *fear lies.*

You can think rationally about a fear and analyze it. The premise is the same: *Fear lies.*

You can experience all the terrible emotions of fear, from mild concern right up to a full panic attack. Nothing changes. *Fear lies.*

152

No matter what you think or feel, no matter how over-whelmingly, fear at its base has no truth to tell you. Fear is not from the Holy Spirit.

More than 365 Scripture verses contain some form of *Do not fear* in them. Pastor Dale says, "God knew we would struggle so much with fear that He gave us one exhortation for each day of the year!"

Whenever the Lord or one of His angels appears to anyone in the Bible, they react with fear. And every time, the Lord or the angel says instantly, "Fear not." With that command comes a powerful peace enabling the hearer to obey.

One day a young Jewish woman was happily going about her daily tasks. Her heart was probably filled with praise and thanksgiving; she was engaged to a wonderful man who would be coming any day now to take her as his bride. Suddenly, with no warning, a massive being of light appeared to her with these words:

> "Greetings, you who are highly favored! The Lord is with you."
>
> [She] was greatly troubled at his words and wondered what kind of greeting this might be. But the angel said to her, "Do not be afraid. . . ."
>
> Luke 1:28–30

Do not be afraid! It was the archangel Gabriel's first command to Mary as he came to tell her the incredible task she had been chosen by God to do.

When God gave commands to His Old Testament servants, He said over and over, "Do not be afraid." Other than the rev-erent fear of knowing the awesome King of the universe, the Creator God, the Judge of all judges, fear is not part of God's *modus operandi* for His children. His perfect love means to cast out all fear (see 1 John 4:18). God does not speak in fear; He enables us to move past it to the peace He alone can give.

Jesus came to show us that God is not a dictator to be feared but a Father who loves and longs to be loved in return.

As I grew older in the Lord, He convicted me that when I let fear or worry into my mind as a thought, or into my heart as an emotion, I am missing the mark of faith. I am sinning. I need to stop and confess those sins and receive some more of that endless forgiveness He offers. The life Jesus came to give me is to be lived by faith and in peace. Fear lies. Fear is not my heavenly Father's voice. Fear is the opposite of faith. God does not speak in a fear.

A Christian's relationship to fear is clearly stated in something I read in an online newsletter recently:

> *No Fear:* It's a popular marketing campaign for a line of teen-oriented products. It's become the slogan of many adrenaline-seeking "extreme sports" participants. But what they don't realize is that this was God's message to us thousands of years before they ever advertised it.
>
> God knew that fear was something His children would consistently struggle with. That's why He reminds us over and over again throughout Scripture that when we are His children, we have nothing to fear. Not anything. . . .
>
> Laura Hepker, *Christianity Online*, June 4, 1999

Ultimately as we grow stronger in our faith, we will consistently do what my friend Ellen Palmer so aptly pointed out one evening a few years ago. Each of us being the mother of four sons, Ellen and I were chronic worriers. So that evening we combed the Bible for passages on fear and worry. I expostulated at some length on the verses we found, while Ellen sat silent.

Finally she grinned at me. "So what you really mean is, we have to turn our *What ifs?* into *So whats!*"

Absolutely, Ellen! We will push past the querulous harassment ("What if this or that happens?") and move on in strengthening faith. We will believe so steadfastly in our Father's love and power that no matter what happens, good or bad, we know He will be working in it all for good (see Romans 8:28). Our acceptance of His will and ultimate purpose of love and blessing enables us to look the *what-if* fear or worry in the face and laugh, "So what? My loving Father has it all in His care."

The Ride of the Vague-aries

Fear has a host of brothers and sisters and cousins who ride with him. If you will excuse a play on Richard Wagner's "Ride of the Valkyries," I call this section "The Ride of the Vague-aries." According to Norse mythology, Valkyries hovered over battlefields, choosing the warriors to be slain. Like them, the "vague-aries" hover over our lives, trying to slay us on the battlefield of faith.

These troublemakers are adept at hamstringing us and keeping us from hearing or obeying the Lord. They have names like *worry, free-floating guilt, anxiety* and *indecision*. Each one of them has a root in fear. The two most common ones are *nebulous fear* (worry) and *vague guilt*.

WORRY

"Do not be anxious about anything," Paul wrote in Philippians 4:6. For me, coming out of a lifetime controlled by fear, this exhortation is another of those wonderful goal Scriptures that we talked about in chapter 2. It shows me the end result of a life lived in constant movement away from worry and into faith.

With all my heart, I believe just what this Scripture implies: I am to learn not to worry or be anxious about a single thing. Not one. When I am concerned, I am to grab those incipient worries and talk them over with my Father before they bloom into weeds that choke my joy.

"But I *have* to worry about my children," you may say. "It's part of being a parent."

It does seem reasonable to entertain concerns about our children—or anyone we love. Heaven knows, they generate worries like ants around a picnic!

"And besides," we reason, "if I didn't worry about my children, I would worry that I wasn't being a good parent."

But our goal is to lift every thought and concern, and any emotion they engender, up to the Lord to see if it is really from Him. And so we have to share these "ants" with the Lord, too. I have found that His love for our loved ones is so far beyond ours that it cannot be measured. He is with them. He cares. We can ask things for them, and petition God with deep emotion, but then it is time to let go and thank God for taking over. We are to walk away from the worry, trusting God to handle it. Turn your *What ifs* into *So whats!*

Bill and I have raised four beloved sons to manhood. Although each has had his share of crises and trials along the way, our number three son, Peter, seems to live perennially like the Peter in the Bible. Life for him is either all up or all down. Remember that fisherman's reaction when Jesus went to wash his feet at the Last Supper? First he refused. Then, when Jesus replied, "Unless I wash you, you have no part with me," Peter exclaimed, "Not just my feet but my hands and my head as well!" (John 13:9).

Our Peter is like that. From birth, life has come to him in huge, all-or-nothing chunks. Often these are exciting chunks; sometimes they are not. Over the years the Lord has used Peter's intense lifestyle to help me understand that it is all right to let go of worry and anxiety about a loved one. I pray often and honestly for Peter, but when I am finished, I picture him covered by a lovely, blood-red rug. Under that cover he is out of my care and control, but safe in his heavenly Father's. I am not allowed to pick up the rug and peek. I move on in peace. If I do find myself mulling over (a nice phrase for worrying about!) Peter, or over any of our sons, I confess that mulling or worry as what it is: sin. More space for grace.

VAGUE GUILT

We have already discussed the problem of guilt versus conviction, but we need to be reminded again and again of the power of vague guilt to keep us from the presence and will of God. Vague guilt is one of the great nasties from the pit of hell. It creeps up on us unawares, sounding pious and thus true. It hides in thoughts like *I probably should have told that person about Jesus* and *By now in my faith walk I ought to be able to control my temper better.*

Shoulds and *oughts* easily become legalisms that breed vague guilt like mosquitoes in stale pondwater.

Nowhere, perhaps, are these vague guilts more prevalent (once again) than in parenting. From the birth of your first-born child, and for the rest of your life, the battle against these pests is endless: *Am I affirming . . . punishing . . . understanding . . . feeding . . . teaching . . . leading . . . this child enough? Too much? Too little? In the right way? In the wrong way? At the right time?*

We fret about our children and about our roles as parents. We brood over our careers and our roles as employers or employees. We worry about our Christian growth and witness. These, and myriads of other worries, unconfessed, become the breeding ground for vague guilt.

We set up fine-sounding standards that may or may not be the Lord's goal for us at that particular time, and when we fail to achieve them, we know we have not sinned, exactly, but it sure feels like it. We are open prey at that point to vague guilt.

It all goes back to taking our thoughts captive and delivering them to Christ. My own prayer often runs like this: "Lord, I am inundated with vague guilt about [whatever]. If there is truth here for me to confess and be forgiven for, then show me clearly. If not, then I accept that I am forgiven, and I am going to walk over these guilts and get on with it." As we learn to take all our thoughts and plans and feelings to the Lord in this way, we will be less blindsided by vague guilt down the road.

As an example, for years vague guilt often nibbled at my heels because I did not seem to be witnessing right. Well, actually I was not doing what I perceived as "witnessing" at all. I never handed out tracts or asked anyone to accept Jesus as his Savior. Only once had I actually prayed with someone to know the Lord, and she had to beg me to do it!

Then our church hosted a day with author Howard Tryon Jr. His book and seminar *Praying for You* (Kregel, 1996) banished my vague guilts about not witnessing "properly." His teaching assured me that only evangelists are called to be evangelists. The rest of us are called to *be* witnesses, to share Christ through our lives and caring prayers first, and be ready, when the time is right, to share in words. My job was to care, pray and be prepared. The rest was the Lord's.

My vague guilts slunk away.

Whatever your personal vague guilts say, there comes a point when each of us needs to affirm boldly, "I am what I am. By God's grace I am a constant sinner constantly forgiven by an incredible God."

Paul said it even better, shouting in the face of the vague guilt being heaped on him by others: "I care very little if I am judged by you or by any human court; indeed, I do not even judge myself. My conscience is clear, but that does not make me innocent. It is the Lord who judges me" (1 Corinthians 4:3–4).

The vague guilts are not God's voice to me. They have no truth to tell. If you hear whispers of guilt in your thoughts, why not open up and share them with the Father? He knows they are there. He will help you know the truth, and the truth will set you free.

"But I Don't Understand!"

God's ways are not our ways and His thoughts are not our thoughts. As vast as the universe towering above our heads, that far beyond our comprehension is the mind of God (see Isaiah

55:9). As my pastor Brent Brooks says, "A god who is small enough for me to understand is not big enough to be God!"

In His wise love, God sometimes answers our prayers in ways that seem incomprehensible. Then He will not tell us why. In the next chapter we will explore two other aspects of the silences of God. Here I want you to think about *our* side of the problem: seeking the wrong information.

"WHY, GOD?"

Why, God? is seldom a good question, and it will seldom get us an answer. Think of all the *whys* we can ask: Why did my child die? Why did Hitler get away with the Holocaust? Why isn't my chronic disease healed? Why hasn't God brought my husband back home? Most of these questions will remain unanswered until we get to heaven.

In her book *Forgiving the Dead Man Walking* (Zondervan, 1998), kidnap and rape victim Debbie Morris writes, "The more 'why' questions I came up with, the more I felt victimized, the more abandoned I felt by God, the more angry I became." The *why* questions Debbie asked alienated her from the presence of the Lord. They encouraged anger and self-pity. (Can you discern the source from which they sprang?) In the course of her powerful book, Debbie recounts how God never answered those questions, but He did bring her back to Himself and heal her ravaged heart and soul. In the end, that was enough.

When we ask, "Why, God?" He can hear and answer the cries beneath that question: "Are You really there? Are You really in control? Do You really love me?"

My friend Linda Kelleher had trouble conceiving and carrying her three girls. Confined to bed in the early weeks of her pregnancies, and medicated and monitored for the rest of the nine months, she had plenty of time to reflect and pray. She also had a terror of losing one of her little ones before birth.

159

"Why, God," she prayed, "can't I just have a normal pregnancy without all this fear and fuss?" But she added another prayer: "Can You show me something that will comfort me if I lose a baby?"

God answered that last cry. One night as she lay awake, He spoke comfort into her heart: *The purpose of life is eternal life.*

The words dropped like a rain shower onto parched earth. Instantly she understood: Whether her child lived for three minutes or three decades or threescore or more years, the purpose of that existence was to find and enjoy eternal life with God. Life here, as pleasant as it can be with friends and family and laughter and love, is nothing compared to life with our heavenly Father. No one who has died and seen Jesus face to face, who has experienced the Love far beyond any earthly love, would ever willingly return to earth. Believers who die in the Lord do not cry or miss us; they live in the full knowledge of God's perfect love, and that whatever He does is right and good, and they wait joyfully for us to join them.

God did not tell Linda why she had to have such difficult pregnancies, but He did answer the cry of her heart for comfort and peace. He also gave her three healthy babies.

It was an affront to me as a new believer (as I mentioned early on) to realize that God's mind is so far beyond mine that He sometimes simply cannot—or will not—cross the chasm so I can understand His thoughts or actions. The Reverend Tom Mackey in Ohio, who mentored Bill into faith in the spring of 1975, suggested to Bill and me that we keep a notebook filled with the unanswerable questions we want to ask the Lord when we see Him. For myself I envision a file cabinet! I open a drawer, stuff my question in as a prayer and slam the drawer shut.

However you do it, it is O.K. to ask God about unanswerable things. And it is O.K. for Him not to tell you now, or ever. He is still God. He is both wise and good. He knows when we frail humans simply cannot understand something in any way He can communicate to us now. Our faith must make up the difference.

THE "NEED TO KNOW" PRINCIPLE

Before I met Bill, he was a Marine intelligence officer. Learning about this part of his life helped me understand the silences of God in another way.

The military has a security regulation called "the need to know." The Commander-in-Chief has a right, theoretically, to know everything from nuclear war codes on down to the number of rolls of toilet paper on order for a particular barracks. His subordinates, on the other hand, operate on a need-to-know basis. If a piece of intelligence pertains directly to administrating a specific mission, a particular subordinate may have access to it. If the superior decides that the subordinate has no need to know—even if he has the proper clearance, or the "right" to know—then the information is withheld. Even so, the subordinate must still obey a direct order unquestioningly, based on the piece of intelligence he or she was not given!

Job 25:3 refers to God as the head of an army. My Commander-in-Chief does indeed know all and is eternally right. My job as one of His subordinates is to follow His orders, whether I am told why or not. There are times in my walk with the Lord when I discern that I must do—or not do—something. I have no rational reason. All I can say is, "Yes, *Sir*," and obey.

Yet I have learned that God's silences are not dark voids. They are filled with love and with the words *Trust Me*. It is in God's great silences (more on them in the next chapter) that I learn to choose intentionally to believe. So I reread Hebrews 11:6: "Without faith it is impossible to please God, because anyone who comes to him must believe that he exists and that he rewards those who earnestly seek him." And I affirm once more to myself that God *is* and that He is a rewarder, a Giver of good gifts and answers, even if I do not perceive them as good until heaven.

DOES GOD EVER SAY THINGS THAT FRIGHTEN US?

When we first come to know the Lord, we begin to perceive His incredible, endless love for us. We start to understand that He is not a whip-brandishing Judge but a Father. We can breathe more easily when we think of the Almighty, and realize that He wants only good for us.

But when we pray and ask for insight or wisdom, will He ever respond with something bad? Jesus addressed this question head-on:

> "Which of you, if his son asks for bread, will give him a stone? Or if he asks for a fish, will give him a snake? If you, then, though you are evil, know how to give good gifts to your children, how much more will your Father in heaven give good gifts to those who ask him!"
>
> Matthew 7:9–11

God will not give us something bad. And if He sends an answer to prayer that seems bad, He will send something good with it: His own Spirit and peace.

The best example I have of this is from my dear friend Sharon Pyle Young. At 45 her husband, Steve, had a massive heart attack. Sharon rode in the ambulance to the hospital that evening, and as they rushed Steve to the ICU for resuscitative care, she ran to the chapel to pray.

"O Lord!" she began, dropping to her knees, "Please, please. . . ."

She planned to say, "Heal Steve," but the words would not come out.

In the instant of space between the spoken and the unspoken, Sharon suddenly felt the warmth of the Lord all around her. She let it flow. After a few minutes she took a deep breath and said, "He isn't going to make it, is he?"

The presence of the Lord was so close that she knew He was saying two things: *No* and, at the same time, *It will be all right.*

God had just relayed to Sharon a hard thing. A bad thing. The worst thing. But His love and comfort and assurance were so powerful that she could accept it, even as the tears began to fall.

After several weeks Steve did die. But Sharon was provided for. She survived the grief. And some years later she married a wonderful man. She was all right.

Many of the end-time passages we read in Matthew 24 and Luke 21 and throughout Revelation—or even prophecy inter-pretation from a source we trust—are similarly frightening. But fear is not from the Lord; it is lying to us. However awful certain end-time events sound to us, nothing will ever tear us away from God's love and provisionary care. Paul wrote "that neither death nor life, neither angels nor demons, neither the present nor the future, nor any powers, neither height nor depth, nor anything else in all creation, will be able to sepa-rate us from the love of God that is in Christ Jesus our Lord" (Romans 8:38–39).

I find no exceptions in that passage. Whether we are here or there when the worst of times comes, we are safe inside the Father's love. Either way we win.

God does say bad things; but they arrive so full of Him-self that terror fades away and pain finds comfort. If you find yourself worried, fearful or panicked over something bad you think you heard from the Lord, ask Him. If the peace does not come, let go of the idea; it is not His. Trust instead in His love.

Once Over Lightly

In learning to discern the Lord's voice, we find there are places and ways He does not speak. He does not speak in doubt or fear. He does not speak in worries

163

or vague guilts that hassle us. He may use these emotions as a "check" to get us to pray and seek Him more before acting, or He may use them just to confirm to us that we are definitely hearing Him. (The very presence of a doubt can mean we were right the first time!) He does want us to root those things out and take them to Him. He will help us turn the *What ifs?* into *So whats!*

Sometimes the Lord does not tell us why something is the way it is; He wants us to believe in Him even when He is silent. He wants us to love and trust and obey Him even if we are not told the reason why, or if the result makes no sense to us.

Occasionally the Lord lets us know potentially frightening or difficult things. But they come with His love and comfort everywhere within them. If there is no peace, it may well not be the Lord telling us the bad thing at all.

All unpleasant things are allowed for at least one good reason: to strengthen our faith. And this is *most* pleasing to Him.

In the next chapter we will look at some of the hindrances we face in discerning the Lord's voice, and some ideas that have helped me and others move past roadblocks.

Your Turn to Discern

1. Analyze one or two doubts that you have entertained recently. Did they sound like the snake hiss of "Did God really . . . ?" What does Scripture say about them? Use a concordance to look up either your central concern or its opposite. Have you talked these doubts over with the Lord? If not, be sure to do so.

2. Are you sometimes hamstrung by fears? Do those fears actually happen? Dig a little deeper with any fears that have come true. Was the surface fear your real one, or were there other fears fueling it from below? Go deeper until you find the place fear lied.

3. What do you worry about most? Why is worry a sin? Read Romans 8:28, 38–39 and make two lists: what God cannot work for good and what can keep us from His love. If both your lists are empty, you have the right answer! What problems in your life can He not work for good?

4. Do you have some vague guilts hanging on in your life? Are they telling you any truth? Ask the Lord.

5. What unanswered *Why?* questions do you have? Share them with your heavenly Father, then let go of them. Let Him handle those questions in His own way and time.

Suggestion: Over the years my prayer partners and I have found a helpful way to get rid of nagging worry, fear and vague guilts. We call it the coffee-can solution. If, after confessing a chronic problem of worry over someone or something, it still hangs on, I actually write it out on a piece of paper, then burn the paper—and the worry—in a coffee can. As I watch the scrap of paper curl up and blacken, I pray, "Lord, I have now given every facet of this problem totally to You. It's gone from my control. You alone can solve it."

When the hassler comes back at me, I can say, "No! On [such-and-such a day at such-and-such a time], I gave [the person or problem] utterly to the Lord. Go talk it over with Him!"

Once you do that, you can turn away freely from those thoughts.

Hindrances and Helps in Hearing the Lord

So you are seeking the Lord's will and praying earnestly, and nothing seems to happen. You sense no words of wisdom or direction in your head or heart. You feel as if you are staring at a blank wall. Or you have heard from the Lord, but suddenly nothing seems to be making His plan or promise come true. What now?

Sometimes hindrances arise to hearing a plan or receiving a promise from the Lord. Occasionally the Lord Himself is simply choosing to be silent or to have you wait. More often you will experience hindrances you get to do something about. You will have to discern which.

Here are some obstacles and helps I have found in my own pilgrimage, to help you get started in discerning and overcoming hindrances.

Hindrances from God

Our God is a great God and He does great things. Sometimes He puts up His own hindrances to our hearing or receiving promises from Him. He does this in great ways, too! I call two of them "the great silence" and "the great wait."

THE GREAT SILENCE

From time to time the Lord simply does not give us a strong indication about which choice is His for us at that moment.

Because I have been a chronic worrier, I usually submit all my travel details to Him; it makes me feel safer. I will ask Him, "Lord, should I take the train or drive? Which train or route shall I take?" I used to receive a peaceful sense of which choices were His plans for me. In recent years, instead of a clear sense of one option, sometimes I will hear only silence. At first these silences frightened me. What was the problem? Had I asked a wrong thing? In the wrong way? I wanted the security of hearing clearly so I could brush past my fears.

But God was teaching me a new thing. He can be a God of "and-and." In cases like this, where there are equal options and neither seems stronger, either option is perfectly all right. I am safe whichever way I do it. If I take the train, He will be with me; if I drive, He will ride right along. For me this has been part of learning to live beyond fear-driven choices and inside the joyous freedom of God's love.

If you are learning to live without fear, this might be why sometimes you get no strong indication of which way is best. He wants you to see that, in His love, you are free to choose.

Sometimes His silence is linked to a "self" or "sin" problem discussed below. But some of His silences, as we saw in the last chapter, are known only to Him. You will have to wait and ask Him in heaven.

THE GREAT WAIT

We also see God's great silence in the great wait. Many times when you have heard and acknowledged a specific plan or dream as coming from God's heart to yours, that dream seems to die. You must undergo a long wait until His promise is fulfilled.

The Bible is full of examples of the great wait. Noah worked on the ark for a century before it began to rain. Abraham and Sarah got so tired of waiting on God's promise for a son that after ten years they thought they were supposed to do something about it themselves—and made a mess of it. Joseph heard God clearly that he was to serve Pharaoh, then languished in prison for several more years until God's time came about. Moses tended his father-in-law's sheep on the back side of nowhere for forty years, yet I think he sensed all the while that there was still something he was meant to do.

My own family, and probably yours, has known long periods of the great wait—times when we knew God had a plan and promise for us, but we did not yet see it. A book like Karen Barber's *Ready, Set, Wait* (Baker, 1996) can encourage you during a long waiting process. So can the Psalms, many of them written while David was running from Saul, in his own great wait between his anointing as king and his ascension to the throne.

Because the great wait occurs so frequently in the Bible, I suspect it is part of God's regular promise process. You can just about count on it, especially if the knowing or promise you have is deeply important to you and others. So don't be surprised if you hear the Lord, and have it confirmed, and then go through a long wait to see it happen. God uses this time to test our faithfulness in believing Him, and in turning ourselves and our honest unbelief over to Him again and again.

In a great wait? Relax back in His arms. Ignore the hissing voice that asks, "Did God *really* say . . . ?" God's promise is God's promise, and whether you pass or fail the hang-in-there test, He will fulfill all He has said. Let Him do it in His way and His time. When it comes, it will be all the sweeter for being His gift to you.

Hindrances You Can Control

Many hindrances to hearing the Lord, unlike the great silence and the great wait, rest under our control. We can trace most of the reasons we do not hear the Lord back to the self life or the sin nature. And the good news is, we can do something about those problems. We can learn to listen, discern and become totally honest with God.

Let's look at just seven of these hindrances. (There are certainly more!) Then you can discern for yourself where your own special hindrances lie.

1. SELF

From the moment we are born, we want what we want, when and how we want it. Learning to want what our heavenly Father wants, and when and how He wants it, requires a whole new way of doing things, starting with rock-bottom honesty with ourselves and with Him. Nowhere is this clearer than in learning to hear His voice—and then choosing to obey it.

Jesus never sinned, but He did struggle with self. "'Father, if you are willing, take this cup from me. . . .' And being in anguish, he prayed more earnestly, and his sweat was like drops of blood falling to the ground . . ." (Luke 22:42, 44).

"This cup" was the agony of the next fifteen hours or so as He was interrogated, beaten, mocked, stripped and nailed to a cross to die a hideously painful, lingering death, separated by our sin from His Father, for nothing that was His fault and for everything that was ours. Three times in the Garden He fell on His face before the Father and begged Him to be willing to keep Him from going through this terrible event.

God was silent. He waited. Jesus struggled with self, with His very human side. Then, three times, He laid that down, too: "Yet not my will, but yours be done" (Luke 22:42).

Your "self" can also be wounded and unable to hear clearly. We can be like damaged radio receivers: The signal is coming to us from the relay tower, but we are broken somewhere inside. The answer, of course, is to ask the Lord to heal you everywhere within. Finding a Christian counselor can help wonderfully.

God longs for you to lay your self down and wait, in peace, for His will, for what He wants or needs to do with you. You may have hurts that need to be healed. You may be struggling with your will, as Jesus did. Just do your best to lay your self down before the Lord and wait. Whatever He gives you, it will be good or it will be worked for good. That is a promise (see Romans 8:28). The Father did not give Jesus what seemed good at the time, yet it was worked for the greatest good that ever was—the reconciliation of all mankind with God.

In dying to your self, you will find life and hear your Father's heart for you.

2. SIN

Isaiah 59:2 says, "Your iniquities have separated you from your God; your sins have hidden his face from you, so that he will not hear." If God is not hearing you, you will not hear back from Him! Unconfessed sin in your life is the greatest hindrance to hearing from the Lord.

Any sin blocks the flow of communication with God. Perhaps the most common one is unforgiveness.

Boy, did I feel that in church one Sunday last summer! It was as if my prayers were bashing themselves to death against the brick walls of the auditorium. My worship was devoid of joy. Then the pastor read the passage for the day, Matthew 5:23–24: "If you are offering your gift at the altar and there remember that your brother has something against you, leave your gift there in front of the altar. First go and be reconciled to your brother. . . ."

Instantly I knew what I had to do—and do right then. Bill and I had been having an ongoing communication problem. Every conversation seemed to end in an argument. I had become so fed up that my heart had grown cold with anger at him. I did not even care that he had skipped church to go to a ham radio event a hundred miles away. Now, looking at my watch, I knew he would be just about at the gate and, once parked, unreachable for hours.

So I slipped out of my seat, raced outside to the pay phone and fumbled for 35 cents. I did not know if I wanted him to answer the cell phone or not, but I had to try.

On the fourth ring he answered.

"Hi, it's me," I said hesitantly.

"O.K. I'm just about to park. What do you want?"

I took a deep breath and cut past weeks of irritation. "Well, the sermon today is based on Matthew 5:24, and I know I have to ask your forgiveness for being so cold and uncaring toward you. I want to be reconciled."

I waited.

Finally Bill spoke, his voice gentler. "Me, too, honey. I'm sorry, too. We'll try harder."

After a few more words I hung up and went back inside. Suddenly my spirit could soar in prayer and worship. I could sense the Lord's love. Forgiveness sought, received and given had opened a clear channel to heaven.

If you are having trouble hearing from the Lord, look for unforgiveness in your life. If you have been wronged, forgive, whether you talk to the person who wronged you or not, whether you do it with great emotion or simply as an act of will. If you need forgiveness, seek it relentlessly. Even if it is not given to you, ask forgiveness from God and then be at peace, enabled to hear from Him.

Any sin that you harbor, or you think you have to harbor because you believe it cannot be forgiven, will keep you from hearing God's loving voice for you. For you as a believer, there is no sin—past, present or future—that He will not forgive. You cannot out-sin His grace.

3. NOT BEING TOTALLY HONEST WITH GOD

We must go deep into the secret places we hide from God and from ourselves and get very honest. Lack of honesty is yet another hindrance to hearing from the Lord.

If there is something you think God might want you to do and you do not want to do it, then tell Him so! Because I have come out of a lifetime of chronic fear, I have learned to be very candid in my prayers: "Lord, please, please, don't ask me to fly [have an anesthetic; face that person; drive the Beltway]. Because I won't do it, and I don't want to disobey You."

My list seemed endless. In His mercy the Lord did not ask me to do those things—at least not while I was held in terror by them. It was like my learning to cross the mountain.

Our oldest son, Tom, decided to attend James Madison University in Harrisonburg, Virginia. That meant that in order to visit him, Bill and I had to cross the Blue Ridge Mountains on a winding, two-lane road with drop-offs on one side.

Even with Bill doing all the driving, I was terrified. I would lie awake half the night before, anticipating that road. My imagination saw our brakes fail, a truck lose control and head straight for us, the car topple over the edge into the valley. The horrible scenarios seemed endless. The next day, as we started up the foothills, I would grasp the door handle until my knuckles turned white and I had to take deep breaths to keep the terror from overcoming me entirely. Going down I was dizzy with fear until we made the final curve and came out onto level roadway once again.

Bill did not understand my irrational behavior, but he was kind about it. As the years went by and we drove it more and

173

more, I loosened my death grip on the handle slightly, and found I could go higher and higher before I hyperventilated, and I could breathe naturally again sooner, going down the other side.

Then our second son, John, not only chose JMU but decided to live in Harrisonburg. That ridge became a permanent part of our lives. After ten years I could actually drive us up the first foothill before turning the car over to Bill.

Then came the day when Bill could not accompany me to Harrisonburg; he needed to be at home and I needed to be there. I would have to drive the mountain myself. I knew the Lord had picked the time to make me face it.

Only a couple of times the night before did a bad scene try to get into my head. I pushed it away and went back to sleep. To me that was miracle enough. But God had more.

Yes, I drove to Harrisonburg. My little gray-green car took herself up those winding roads like a mountain goat. At the top I slowed to a crawl, put her into second gear and took a great breath. Down we went into the turns—and suddenly I found myself crying in joy. I was driving the mountain and I was not afraid! Winking back the tears, I sang all the way down.

I had been honest with God all along, and in His slow, gentle way He had changed me. He did not ask me to try to drive the mountain to overcome my fear. He preferred mercy to that kind of sacrifice. But He removed the fear, step by step, and turned the mountain into a molehill. Then He asked me to drive the molehill.

Don't be afraid to be honest with God. Tell Him the whole thing—what you do and do not want, what you really think or feel about something. If you are unwilling, tell Him you are willing to be made willing, if you are. If you are not, ask Him to make you willing, or willing to be willing. Your own willpower can be a major hindrance to hearing the Lord. Throw yourself into His arms and let Him take care of it all. Father knows best.

4. GRUMBLING

Praise was the golden key that unlocked the door of my life so the Lord could come in and change it.

One night in March 1974, I was up late rocking Peter. He was suffering with one of his chronic earaches. Even when he was not hurting, he was a poor sleeper, and I had gone two years with few nights of unbroken rest. I was perpetually tired, frustrated and angry. I rocked furiously as he whimpered. None of the boys had ever seemed comfortable in my arms, and he had been no exception.

Then he gave a little shudder and fell asleep. His warm little body relaxed into mine. I stared down at him. Unexpected gentleness washed over me. Without even thinking, I began to whisper, "Thank You for this child! Thank You for him!" I am not sure I knew whom I was thanking, but something in me had melted, and I needed to give thanks.

Suddenly I sensed incredible warmth all around me. Peter, the rocker and I were enveloped in great peace. I sat there for a few minutes as it faded, then put my son into his crib and went back to bed.

That small moment of praise made way for the big moment a month later when the Lord walked into my life and turned it upside-down. One of the first promises that I made to Him: that as far as I was able or enabled, I would always praise Him in and for all things in my life.

One of the fastest ways I lose communication with the Lord, therefore, is when I grumble—a fourth hindrance to hearing from God.

Grumbling is not talking *with* the Lord; it is talking *about* Him. Here are excerpts from the classic chapter on grumbling and its results:

> The people complained about their hardships in the hearing of the LORD, and when he heard them his anger was aroused. Then fire from the LORD burned among them and

consumed some of the outskirts of the camp. . . . The rabble with them began to crave other food, and again the Israelites started wailing and said, "If only we had meat to eat!" . . . The LORD became exceedingly angry, and Moses was troubled. . . . [The LORD said to Moses:] "Tell the people: '. . . The LORD heard you when you wailed, "If only we had meat to eat! We were better off in Egypt!" Now the LORD will give you meat, and you will eat it. You will not eat it for just one day, or two days, or five, ten or twenty days, but for a whole month—until it comes out of your nostrils and you loathe it—because you have rejected the LORD, who is among you, and have wailed before him, saying, "Why did we ever leave Egypt?"'" . . . While the meat was still between their teeth and before it could be consumed, the anger of the LORD burned against the people, and he struck them with a severe plague. Therefore the place was named Kibroth Hattaavah, because there they buried the people who had craved other food.

Numbers 11:1, 4, 10, 18–20, 33–34

Ultimately a whole generation lost the blessing God had wanted for them:

> You grumbled in your tents. . . . When the LORD heard what you said, he was angry and solemnly swore: "Not a man of this evil generation shall see the good land I swore to give your forefathers. . . ."

Deuteronomy 1:27, 34–35

And they did not.

Grumbling or complaining "in your tent" about something the Lord has done is serious business to Him. It denies His goodness and wisdom, which are far beyond what we can know. Grumbling exposes our selfish rebellion, for which we do not seek forgiveness.

Job, on the other hand, spoke out angry words in his trial of faith. Honest about his anguish, he cried out things such as "Why did I not perish at birth?" (3:11) and "Sighing comes to me instead of food. . . . What I feared has come upon me. . . . I have no peace, no quietness . . . only turmoil" (3:24–26).

Job was honest. He was in God's face about what he felt and thought, yet he did not grumble behind God's back. He told it to the Lord as it seemed to him—and he always came back to glorifying God. "In all this, Job did not sin in what he said" (2:10).

Have you been grumbling about something? It will hinder your discernment. Be honest with God. Talk with Him face to face and pour out your feelings, good and bad. Grumbling is talking behind His back, accusing Him of not being nice to you, of not being fair, of giving you more that you can handle. It is saying things about Him that are not true. Grumbling will cut your communion with the Lord instantly.

Asking forgiveness for it and praising Him will restore that broken communion just as quickly. (More on praise in the next section.)

5. Our Expectations

We may have very scriptural preconceptions about what God will say or how or when He will do something, but those expectations can come between us and how He actually reveals Himself.

My friend Dixie Merrill (one of the three women leading the Bible study that I was disrupting) once had a vision of a garden filled with stones carved in various shapes. "I realized those stones were my expectations of how something should be, or how it ought to happen," she explained. "And then God showed me that those expectations could become idols, or gods before God."

Until then it had never occurred to me that, as a Christian, I could violate the second commandment. But more and more I saw how true Dixie's vision was. My expectations, too, can become graven images etched in my mind that I refuse to give up in order to see or hear the real God.

One example might be what you think someone you love will say or do when he or she becomes a Christian. Often we think that person will sound like us, or grow up in the Lord in the same way we have. If she does not meet that expectation, we may doubt she is really hearing the Lord. Yet God matures each of us on our own unique schedule. Because He does not come to a loved one in the ways we expect, it is not she but we who are not perceiving the Lord. As another example, recall Jonah and his petulant anger because God did not go ahead and destroy those pagan Ninevites. The prophet refused to give up his preconceptions of what God should do.

Many times over the years I have had to stop and ask forgiveness for letting my expectations keep me from hearing or seeing the Lord in some situation. When I do lay down my graven-image expectations (good or bad), I am open to receiving what Dixie calls "the unexpected serendipities of God"—His creative surprises. (And I love surprises!)

6. BEING TOO BUSY

We live in a distracted world. Everyone is so busy that we seldom have time to do anything wholeheartedly—especially listen for an invisible God. Sometimes my mind races at a million miles a second and gets me nowhere. Then I have to stop and say, "Lord, I'm sorry. My mind is a maelstrom today. I want to focus on You. I can't. Please help me." Sometimes all I can do is grit my teeth and silently cry, *Help, Lord!*

You can do this, too, right where you are, inside yourself, in the middle of a crowd, in a meeting, chasing a toddler or wherever you begin to feel rattled, frazzled or irritated. It takes only a second to turn your mind and heart toward Him. He is right there, waiting.

Psalm 37:7 says, "Be still before the LORD and wait patiently for him." Psalm 46:10 adds, "Be still, and know that I am God." I am still learning to center myself down to the still, small voice; to that peace place deep within where His Spirit resides. It is an ongoing process. When I make it, what joy!

7. SOMETHING FOR MARRIED MEN: INSENSITIVITY TO YOUR SPOUSES

In the "Helps for Hearing" section that follows, I offer a suggestion that is special for women, but here is a hindrance to hearing God applicable to married men: "Husbands, . . . be considerate as you live with your wives, and treat them with respect as the weaker partner and as heirs with you of the gracious gift of life, so that nothing will hinder your prayers" (1 Peter 3:7).

If you are not hearing from the Lord, ask Him if your discernment is being affected because you are not cherishing your wife in ways that are important to her. This Scripture is clear that your prayers can and will be hindered if your relationship with her is not mutually considerate, respectful and kind. It was written by Peter, who had a wife (since we know from Matthew 8:14 that he had a mother-in-law). I have a hunch that Peter learned this truism, like so many things in his life, the hard way. But learn it he did—wonderfully enough to share it with us.

If you do not understand your wife's needs, ask the Lord. He created her; He knows what she wants, even sometimes when she does not, and can whisper it into your heart. Or ask her—and really listen.

Helps for Hearing

There are other hindrances to hearing the Lord, as I said. Two that often hamper me are self-pity and anger. But you get the idea.

Meanwhile, here are seven suggestions to help you get past them. These have worked for me in my life of learning to hear

179

the Lord. They include the obvious and the not-so-obvious, as you will see.

1. BECOME A PRAY-ER

Without what we call prayer, we would have no two-way communication with God!

Soon after I came to know Him, I began to read wonderful books about praying. The title of one by Rosalind Rinker, *Prayer: Conversing with God* (Zondervan, 1959), set the tone for my prayer life. Prayer, I learned, is not just a hands-folded or on-my-knees activity. It is not just grace before a meal or reciting the Lord's Prayer (which is really not a prayer at all, but a pattern for prayer). Nor is it only limitless praise or thanksgiving. Prayer is neither just a list of things I want or need, nor interceding for other people or for events or places. Prayer is all of these, of course. But most of all it is a lifelong, lifestyle-changing conversation with the holiest of Gods who also happens to be my Father and my best Friend.

My goal Scripture for prayer is three words: "Pray without ceasing" (1 Thessalonians 5:17, KJV). Over the years I have learned that all kinds of prayers, prayed in any place or way, can move me along toward this goal. Like a parent encouraging a child to walk, the Lord stands before me, hands outstretched, beckoning me to launch out and move toward Him—one prayer, two prayers, ten prayers at a time.

Prayer is turning my thoughts toward my heavenly home. It is interrupting a daydream or wish to make it a prayer. It is stopping a thought process to discuss it with the Lord. It is turning the monologue in my head into a dialogue. It is teaching myself "God-consciousness."

2. EXERCISE GOD-CONSCIOUSNESS

A few weeks ago I traveled north for my mother's ninetieth birthday. On the seven-hour train trip I had time to chat with the Lord alone, to let Him bring to mind other trips along the route and to show me how far He has brought me over the years. Suddenly I realized how easy I now found it to sense God in new places.

But it was not always this way. When I first became a believer, I could usually find the Lord in the living room of our house in Ohio. When I was busy and suddenly felt He was not real, I could go there for a few minutes and whisper, "Lord?" Soon I would sense His presence. But take me not very far from there, or from the fellowship of my believing friends, and I felt lost. It was as if God had died and gone away.

The real problem was not that He was not there, but that I was not yet conscious of His omnipresence. That awareness had to be learned. One book that helped me more than any other to know I can feel, hear and worship God wherever I am is Brother Lawrence's *Practice of the Presence of God* (Whitaker, 1982, and other editions). If you have never read this little book written four hundred years ago by a lay brother in a monastery, please do. It is the perfect starting place for a life of awareness of the Lord.

Practicing God's presence is exactly what you do to become God-conscious. The result is like being a newlywed and experiencing the still-unexpected joy of finding the other person there next to you in the morning—and then becoming an oldy-wed, where that presence is not a surprise but rather the happy norm.

Seek Him. If you are in a new place or situation and think, *Oh, dear, I don't feel the Lord at all. Isn't He here?* just turn the question into a prayer. Ask Him to enable you to sense Him there. Accept that He is.

Over months and years of practice you will find Him everywhere—even in places that make you uncomfortable, or that seem dangerous, or that are just plain boring. He may keep you *in* the world, but He will also enable you not to be *of* it. He will be there with you and you will know it.

My prayer partner, Ellen Palmer, is a born homemaker. She loves to cook and tend to the needs of the men in her life. But as their sons approached college age, her husband, Roger, asked her to find a job. Understanding the reason, but reluctantly, she went to work as the insurance referral coordinator in a doctor's office. For many months Ellen and I prayed that the Lord would somehow make it possible for her to come back home, where her heart was.

Then the Lord showed her that she was working for a reason beyond the extra income. As He nudged her, she began to intercede for the patients whose charts she handled each day, for the people in the office and for those she contacted by phone. Her routine became a place where the Lord met her and where she found her worth in a secret ministry with Him. His blessings flowed through her intercession into the lives of others, and Ellen found His presence in the midst of humdrum work.

Practicing God's presence means that I stop my whirlwind activities whenever I think of it and consciously turn my heart and mind toward Him. I set the compass of my life toward Jesus and wait a moment until my needle stops jiggling. I wait until I hear Him or am aware of Him.

3. LISTEN FOR GOD

Every day since April 1974, I have had some time of quiet with the Lord, in prayer and in Scripture. Sometimes this has been a very set time; in other seasons it has had to be on the fly or scattered throughout a day—or night. Many people call this, as I did for years, their quiet time. But the Lord used Becky Tirabassi's book *Let Prayer Change Your Life* (Nelson, 1990) to change my quiet time. Now I call it my listening time.

Armed with a version of the sectioned notebook Becky suggests, I spend my first minutes each morning with pen in hand, Bible open, listening. I listen for what the Lord wants me to praise and pray. I listen through a Bible chapter for what He intends for me to learn, and for what questions I can jot down for Him to answer. I listen to my own thoughts and try to take them captive as honest written prayers. I listen for what special things God wants me to pray on my daily intercession list. I usually have several notes written in these sections so far. Then at the end I just sit. And I listen.

Catherine Marshall, in the book *Come into His Light* (Revell, 1995), found "that the inner Voice is more likely to speak to me at the first moment of consciousness upon awakening, or during some odd moment during the day as I go about routine tasks, than while I wait expectantly with pad and pencil in hand."

I can say a hearty *Amen!* to that. My listening journal shows precious few jottings in my "Sit Still and Listen" section. My mind wanders. Sometimes I doze off. Nonetheless I still do it for those last few listening-time minutes each morning. And I pull myself back toward heaven throughout the day by saying, "Father, I'm here. I'm still listening."

It is a small beginning.

4. BE FAITHFUL IN SMALL THINGS

If you are not sure how to begin to hear the Lord, start with something small. Ask Him how you can help your spouse after work today, or what to prepare for dinner tonight. When an idea emerges, thank Him. Then do it!

One of the principles of God's Kingdom is that if you are faithful in small stuff, He will make you faithful with big stuff (see Luke 19:11–27). If you practice listening for and obeying Him in the seemingly unimportant details of everyday life, then when big things come along, you will find it easier to hear His plan. Remember the mug the Lord nudged me to take with me to the mall? Small things, big beginnings.

5. WALK IN THE LIGHT YOU HAVE

Sometimes we have to continue doing what we know clearly is the Lord's will, and wait for more revelation or enabling before we move on. During those times follow what Philippians 3:16 says: "Let us live up to what we have already attained." In other words, walk in the light you have.

Dave Goetz, editor of *The Church Leadership Net Newsletter,* suggests that when we are uncertain about what the Lord wants in the long run, we should zoom in on what His plan is for us right now. "When in doubt about your next step," he concludes, "refocus on what you know for certain."

Suppose you have discerned ways you are not being kind or gentle or self-controlled or some other scriptural goal. Convicted of the impossibility of achieving any lasting success in this area, you ask your heavenly Father to enable you to be more like Jesus in this way. After some time you realize you are definitely being kinder or gentler, even in those familiar, anger-producing circumstances. But there are still huge gaps between what you see in yourself and what you think of as perfection. You seem to have reached a plateau and can get no higher. What do you do?

Just keep on walking in the knowledge you have. Like a builder constructing a form to fill with cement, continue to set up the form of kindness or gentleness as best you can. Perform kind acts. Think kind thoughts. Do what you can do on any given day in any given situation. Seek forgiveness for lapses. Ask the Lord for more of His nature. And, most important, don't condemn yourself, either now or in the future, for the enabling you do not yet have. Eventually the Lord will come along and continue filling your "form," not with cement but with the solid gold of His own nature.

And, yes, if your goal is to be the perfect mate or parent, He will protect your spouse or children as you bumble about. He planned their growth in Him to coincide with what you are learning, and yours to coincide with what they are. He will work it *all* for good, for all of you. Give Him time.

In the meantime, walk in the light you have and thank Him for it.

6. PRAISE GOD

We all like the shortest, fastest way to get somewhere. We take shortcuts and avoid the most trafficked patterns. Even our computers are designed with shortcut keys—the quickest ways to perform a function or get a program up and working. Other methods do the same thing but take a few keystrokes (and milliseconds!) longer.

The best spiritual shortcut I have ever found is praise. It has been the lovely key over the last 25 years—ever since that late night rocking Peter—that has unlocked dark doors and led me straight out into the light. It sets me on an even keel in an emotional storm. It creates "heavenly static" when my mind is filled with wild thoughts I know are from the enemy. It fills me with peace when I feel as if I cannot find the Lord at all.

I have praised Him when I felt like it, and while stomping up and down the road to calm my anger at Him or at someone else. I have praised the Lord in joy and laughter, in tears and with my teeth clenched, by an act of will. No matter whether I do it from thankfulness I actually feel or as a true sacrifice of praise, when I feel nothing, it pleases His heart. Praise is a wonderful gift of God—the fastest way to delight Him and to move us past ourselves and out into new realms of faith.

Praise also helps when we realize that our minds have gone off on a tangent. For example, I am a prodigious daydreamer. I can get lost in the most wonderful scenarios, only to realize that I am no longer linked to the reality the Lord has given me. At that point I turn my thinking into thanking. The vowels tell the story: I take out the big *I* in *think* and go with the big *A* in *thank*—as in "Ahhh, Lord, aren't You awesome!" Giving thanks for something, whether related to my daydream or not, turns my heart immediately back toward the Lord; my thoughts soon follow. I have taken them captive.

May I suggest a small test of praise? The next time you whack your thumb with a hammer or hit your crazy bone or slice your finger with a paper cut, instead of whatever you usually say, try praising God. Bless and thank Him instead of howling or maybe even saying something unpleasant. You will feel ridiculous, but you will be in for a surprise.

Praise opens up the doors between you and heaven. It brings God into the situation. It moves you beyond you. The situation may not change at all, but you will be changed in it.

7. SOMETHING SPECIAL FOR WOMEN

If you are a married woman, I have an extraordinary challenge for you in these modern times: You can listen for the Lord through your husband! If you are unmarried, you can listen for Him through your pastor or father or brother or any special Christian man He has put into your life. In His infinite wisdom God planned for us women to have an extra way to hear Him—through the men who care for us.

Maybe part of the reason for this special concern is that God created men and women to respond differently to the same situations. About four months along in the womb, a boy baby receives a wash of chemicals over the right side of his brain that baby girls do not get. This leaves males with the rational cortex the predominant one, predisposing them to respond less emotionally in situations than a woman might. It gives men the ability to remain calmer in an emergency than women sometimes do. And in their calmness we women can find stability.

If God has given you a "covering," caring male, by all means read Ephesians 5:22–24, Colossians 3:18 and 1 Peter 3:1, and talk to the Lord about the idea of hearing Him through your husband or whomever He has provided. Then, when you need specific guidance, ask that man what you want to know. Expect his prayerful response to be the Lord's and, because it will be the Lord's answer, plan to follow it.

Tip for a married woman: When you submit a problem to your husband for guidance, if you think or know he is wrong in what he decides (even after you have told him so gently and honestly), do not be afraid to go along. The Lord can handle both him and the outcome, and protect you in the process. Recall Sarah in 1 Peter 3:6, Genesis 12:11–20 and Genesis 20:1–18. Pray for the Lord to help you discern how this applies in your own marriage relationship.

What a wonderful gift caring men are to us women to help us hear the Lord more clearly! As a new believer I used this gift all the time to make sure I was hearing God correctly. It blew my husband away. Actually, it blew him right out of agnosticism and into faith! I still expect to hear Him through Bill—even when (as in the selection of photos of our son Tom) I don't always bother to listen.

Jesus listened, too. In the final chapter we will see how He did it, and, by His grace, has shown through others before us how we may yet do it.

Once Over Lightly

As much as we want to hear the Lord's voice, and as much as He wants us to, we usually encounter hindrances. Sometimes they are God's silences or waits. More often we are hindered by the stumblingblocks of our own selves and of sin. If we are honest and uncomplaining, we can discern the problem and seek forgiveness and whatever else we need. We *will* eventually hear Him!

We can practice prayer and His presence. We can be in the Scriptures every day with a listening ear. We

can be faithful in small things. We can walk in the
light we have, and practice praise. And we can hear
Him in those God has given to care for us.

---

your turn to discern Your Turn to Discern

1. What are your own personal hindrances to hearing
God? How do these fit into the categories in this chapter?

2. Have you experienced a great silence or a great
wait? How did you handle it?

3. Have you had expectations or preconceptions that
kept you from hearing the Lord? Do you have some
now? Have you been angry at Him, as Jonah was,
because He did not do something the way you wanted
Him to? Confess these "graven images" to Him, lay your
own expectations down and watch for the unexpected
serendipities of God!

4. Reread Paul's letters to the Ephesians and Philippians. Make special note of places you find the words *joy*
and *praise* and *thanks* or *thanksgiving*. Ask the Lord how He
wants you to apply these qualities in your life.

5. What helps have you found to hearing the Lord
more clearly?

Suggestion: Keeping certain Scriptures handy, posted
in your work area or over your kitchen sink, can help
stop an angry response and turn your heart toward what
the Lord wants to say, either to you or to others.

One effective passage condenses what the Lord's voice
will sound like: "The wisdom that comes from heaven is
first of all pure; then peace-loving, considerate, submissive, full of mercy and good fruit, impartial and sincere.
Peacemakers who sow in peace raise a harvest of righ-

teousness" (James 3:17–18). Another passage tips us off as to where to put our thoughts when they are rambling or fuming: "Whatever is true, whatever is noble, whatever is right, whatever is pure, whatever is lovely, whatever is admirable—if anything is excellent or praiseworthy—think about such things" (Philippians 4:8).

Glimpses of Our Goal

In recent years, as Charles Sheldon's novel, *In His Steps,* reached the century mark, the question around which the book centers has become a modern icon. The letters *WWJD* have turned up on bumper stickers, keychains, bracelets. In the story, "What would Jesus do?" (WWJD) is the challenge given to a group of everyday men and women who, for one year, are to approach every decision with this query in mind. It is a wonderful question for all of us to ask, all our lives—a basic question of discernment.

I would like to add a second question to it: "What would Jesus say?" I do not mean this in the sense of a finger-wagging "Now, what would Jesus say about your doing that?" but, literally, an encouraging "What would Jesus say now, in this situation, to you or through you?" Learning to discern the voice of God for every action or thought is a lifelong process. Our ultimate goal is to become like Jesus—to know what He wants us to do and say in each moment of our lives.

In this last chapter let's first look at Him, and then catch glimpses of how He has revealed Himself to some of us now, and through some who have kept the faith before us.

How Did Jesus Do It?

How did Jesus hear and communicate with the Father? One of the best examples comes from the football field.

For several seasons our oldest son, Tom, had a weekend job working field security for the Denver Broncos. What a joy it was for him to be a small part of the organization through two Super Bowl wins! Once in a while I caught a glimpse of him on the left side of our TV screen, back to the field, monitoring the crowd up near one of the goalposts.

Over the seasons I became aware that some sideline coaches wore headsets. From whom were they getting information? To whom were they talking? And about what? Curious, I e-mailed Tom.

"I think it depends on the coach," he wrote back. "Some listen to the back-and-forth of their chief assistants, such as the offensive and defensive coordinators and the special teams coach. Many times the coordinator sits in the boxes above the field because it gives him a better view. If he doesn't, one of his assistants does. Information such as 'Jones looks as if he is hurt' or 'the enemy's offensive line seems to be working the right side more' is relayed to the coaches on the sidelines. NFL coaches can then call the plays directly to the quarterback on the field through a low-powered radio transmission. The quarterback has a small receiver and speaker in his helmet. . . ."

What a great picture of how Jesus discerned and shared! High above, His Father, the great Coordinator, saw the big picture. He spoke truth into Jesus' heart, and Jesus passed to the team on the field—His disciples—exactly what He heard His Father saying. Over and over in the gospel of John, Jesus is clear about this:

"I do nothing on my own but speak just what the Father has taught me" (John 8:28). "I did not speak of my own accord, but the Father who sent me commanded me what to say and how to say it. . . . Whatever I say is just what the Father has told me to say" (John 12:49–50). "The words I say to you are not just my own. Rather, it is the Father, living in me, who is doing his work. . . . These words you hear are not my own; they belong to the Father who sent me" (John 14:10, 24).

As Jesus listened for God's voice, He discerned it perfectly. Whatever He spoke to others came straight from God's heart to their ears. This is because He was one—a single unit or essence—with His Father (see John 14:9–10). Their communication was unbroken.

Yet Jesus was also fully man. When He spoke to the Lord on His own behalf, He was completely human and poured out His heart. (Recall His cries in Gethsemane and on the cross.) But when Jesus was speaking to others, He always said just what He heard from His Father.

We are the children of the same Father. Our Lord and Savior, Jesus, is also our big Brother, and we are meant to grow up to be like Him. Romans 8:29 affirms that "those God foreknew he also predestined to be conformed to the likeness of his Son, that he might be the firstborn among many brothers." Over the years of our growth in faith, we can expect to begin to act and react more and more like Jesus, and begin consistently to hear the Father. Will we ever have perfect, instantaneous discernment, as Jesus did? No, not here on earth; but we can still grow toward that goal. And we do not do it alone.

One of the things Jesus heard from the Coordinator and passed on to the disciples (and us) is that "when he, the Spirit of truth, comes, he will guide you into all truth. He will not speak on his own; he will speak only what he hears . . ." (John 16:13). This means we have the same access to the voice of God that Jesus had. The living Spirit of God resides deep within our beings. Like the Broncos quarterback, we, too, can hear a voice in our helmets.

What a wonderful hope as we grow in hearing the Lord! We will be able to distinguish His from other voices, as Jesus promised as He spoke of Himself as the Shepherd: "His sheep follow him because they know his voice. But they will never follow a stranger; in fact, they will run away from him because they do not recognize a stranger's voice" (John 10:4–5). The voice in our helmets will become so familiar that should another coach try to scramble or duplicate our Coach's voice, we will discern it immediately and not obey. We will even run in the opposite direction.

To grow in this grace of discernment, we need to turn on and tune in our receiver, listening over the roar of the crowd and the taunts of the opposition for the quiet, all-knowing voice of our Coach.

So What Does God's Voice Sound Like?

I don't know! Nobody does. Yet we know that we can and do hear it, and that we can learn to discern it from all the other voices that clamor around us—our own, the voices of the world and the voice of the enemy. But we cannot describe God's voice, as we can the voices of people around us, because we do not usually hear it with our ears. It comes through the Holy Spirit kindling our spiritual senses—our hearts and minds. It can also come as events or actions instead of words.

Like shafts of sunlight through a dense forest, God's voice shines through differently every time. Here are some reminders of how His voice can come to us.

NOT ALWAYS AS WE EXPECT

We saw in the last chapter that our expectations can easily become hindrances to hearing. God gets to choose how He will reveal Himself.

Have you heard the old joke about the drowning man who cried out to God to save him? He shooed away another boater, the Coast Guard and a rescue helicopter, then sank and died. When he saw the Lord in heaven, he asked, "Hey, I asked You to save me and You didn't! How come?"

"Whom do you think sent the boater, the Coast Guard and the helicopter?" was God's reply.

AN UNUSUAL REACTION IN A CRISIS

Sometimes God's voice does not come in words, but through uncommon actions or reactions.

One night recently my friend Janice Ferguson's daughter, Felicia, was driving an unfamiliar route home from a movie. Within minutes rain was pelting the car. Aware of a severe storm warning, she began to pray earnestly. Then the wind buffeted the car so fiercely that she brought it to a full stop right in the middle of the deserted road. In the next second a huge tree crashed down in front of the car. An instant later, unbelievably, a second large tree smashed down just behind her.

Instead of opening the car door and leaning or stepping out (a natural reaction!), Felicia sat still until the wind and downpour lessened. Then, still without cracking her door, she reached up and slid open the moon roof. Peering out, she saw electrical wires draped over and around her vehicle, trailing into the puddles.

Because of her sudden stop and uncanny wisdom in not doing the natural thing, Felicia remained unharmed as she waited calmly for help to arrive.

"I'm not sure where the discernment came from," she says. "I had the knowledge when I needed it."

Felicia perceived no voice and felt no presence, yet she heard the Lord. Her prayers prepared her for Him. His voice came as the peace and calm knowledge of what to do, and not do, in a life-threatening situation.

AN ALMOST-AUDIBLE INTERJECTION

Remember the "nudges with teeth" in chapter 8—when God sometimes gives us a shove? These experiences are usually the closest we will come to hearing an audible voice from God.

"I'm just learning how to listen to the Lord," Susan Tomaselli began as she shared a story with our Thursday Bible study group recently. "Last Thursday I was disappointed that my co-worker Cassandra didn't visit our Bible study, as she had said she would. I've been witnessing to her for over a year, and I really wanted her to meet all of you. Well, Friday morning I went to the gym to train. I was in the middle of a set of exercises when I heard a voice in my head saying, *Call Cassandra now and ask her to pray to receive Christ.*

"I have never done that with anyone in my life! I certainly didn't plan to start with Cassandra. She and I are co-workers, but I wouldn't say we're close friends. Thinking my mind was playing tricks on me, I dismissed the command and continued to train. Suddenly I saw a picture of Jonah and the whale in my head. Again I heard: *Call Cassandra now and ask her to pray to receive Christ.* I definitely didn't want to get swallowed by a whale! So I stopped my workout and ran for the phone. The whole time I was thinking, *She won't be home and I'll be off the hook.*

"She answered on the third ring. I asked her if she'd read the tracts I'd left on her desk. She said she had. I asked her if she'd prayed to receive Christ. She said she didn't think she would know how. Then I asked her if she would like me to pray with her. She said yes. It was a simple, heartfelt prayer guided by the Holy Spirit. We now have a new sister in Christ!"

I e-mailed Susan and asked what that inner voice sounded like to her. She wrote back:

"It felt like a thought in the shape of a full sentence: *Call Cassandra now and ask her to pray to receive Christ.* It broke into my immediate train of thought, which was along the line of *That's right, just one more rep, good form, keep it smooth.* Cassandra was nowhere on my mind till I got that nudge. Still, I dismissed it and got back on track with *Finish the set, back training's almost over, move on to biceps.*

"The next time the nudge came it was harder and more distinct. Thoughts of Jonah flashed through my mind. I knew if I didn't stop right away and make the phone call, I would be acting in direct disobedience to God. I knew it was His prompting, because making a call like that was so out of character for me."

The voice was not audible—but it was as clear as if it had been.

MORE DISCERNIBLE WITH PRACTICE

At the end of the e-mail, Susan wrote wistfully, "Does hearing the Lord get easier with practice?"

My friend Janice Ferguson, from that long-ago Bible study, had talked with me recently about this very question. I like the way she put it:

"Discernment, listening with comprehension, is a skill. God gives us the frequency—His Holy Spirit. But sometimes we get interference with the reception. As new listeners we are so plugged in to the Source that every event is a miracle. At that point we don't know how to tune in the frequency, so we hear everything. Sometimes it's so overpowering that we have to turn it down. The problem is, if we turn it too low or shut it off altogether, it may take a while to find the frequency again.

"Discernment is a skill that must be practiced, because it grows. It is built on faith, trust and past experiences with God's ability to make all things work together for good. My favorite story about discernment is Abraham's servant sent back to the home country to find a wife for Isaac. The part I focus on regarding discernment is: 'I being in the way, the LORD led me . . .' (Genesis 24:27, KJV). That's discernment!—practicing the presence of God daily so that He and we are on the same wavelength."

Janice's thoughts from her decades-long life in the Lord can encourage Susan as she just begins to discern. In the same way, all of us can find encouragement from those who have kept the faith and gone on ahead of us.

Glimpses from Those Who Discerned before Us

We talked in chapter 2 about the race we are running and the fact that we "are surrounded by such a great cloud of witnesses" in the grandstands cheering us on (Hebrews 12:1). But as a new Christian I paid little attention to those who had gone before me in the faith—like a child thinking right now is all that matters. Recently, however, I have come to appreciate not only the saints (believers) in the Old and New Testaments, but also those who have fought the good fight during the centuries since.

Daily Strength for Daily Needs, a devotional compiled a century ago by Mary Tileson, weaves each day's thoughts around a single passage of Scripture, embellished by excerpts from long-gone writers. Her book was a catalyst for me to seek out and read more from elder brothers and sisters who have finished the race. Sometimes the wording or spelling makes me slow down and reread a section; but what incredible comfort comes as I realize that these people struggled to hear and obey and love God just as I do. And they succeeded! Their lives of faith and discernment have stood the test of time and Scripture, and have produced sweet fruit in the lives of millions of believers.

Here are seven excerpts, each one on some aspect of discernment we have covered in preceeding chapters. Unless otherwise noted, these quotations from saints who have passed on are from Tileson's compilation.

RENEWING YOUR MIND

In chapter 3 we discussed why it is necessary to let the Lord renew our thinking to His standard. From Psalm 51:6: "Surely you desire truth in the inner parts; you teach me wisdom in the inmost place."

Hannah Whitall Smith (1832–1911) was the wife of an American evangelist who fell away from God and was unfaithful to her. One of their daughters married Bertrand Russell, well-known British philosopher and atheist. Out of the crucible of her life, she wrote books that have mentored a century of believers. Summing up the depth of our renewal in the Lord, she wrote:

> Anything allowed in the heart which is contrary to the will of God, let it seem ever so insignificant, or be it ever so deeply hidden, will cause us to fall before our enemies. Any root of bitterness cherished towards another, any self-seeking, any harsh judgments indulged in, any slackness in obeying the voice of the Lord, and doubtful habits or surroundings, any one of these things will effectually cripple and paralyse our spiritual life.

We must take it *all* captive to Christ.

FALLING OR FAILING?

Because each of us is a combination of saint and sinner, we are going to fail as we learn to discern. But every time God's grace will be there to forgive us. We do not need to give up, but to press on.

François de Salignac de La Mothe Fénelon (1651–1715) was a French prelate and spiritual mentor to many. He exhorted them:

> Do not be discouraged at your faults; bear with yourself in correcting them, as you would with your neighbour. Lay aside

this ardour of mind, which exhausts your body, and leads you to commit errors. Accustom yourself gradually to carry prayer into all your daily occupations. Speak, move, work, in peace, as if you were in prayer, as indeed you ought to be. Do everything without excitement, by the spirit of grace. As soon as you perceive your natural impetuosity gliding in, retire quietly within. . . . Listen to the leadings of grace, then say and do nothing but what the Holy Spirit shall put in your heart. . . .

ERRING ON THE SIDE OF OBEDIENCE

I have learned that it is better to make a mistake while trying to obey rather than to do nothing. The French theologian Jean-Nicholas Grou (1730–1803) agreed:

If [the committed Christian] falls into some error, he does not fret over it, but rising up with a humble spirit, he goes on his way anew rejoicing. Were he to fall a hundred times in the day, he would not despair,—he would rather cry out lovingly to God, appealing to His tender pity. The really devout man has a horror of evil, but he has a still greater love of that which is good; he is more set on doing what is right, than avoiding what is wrong. Generous, large-hearted, he is not afraid of danger in serving God, and would rather run the risk of doing His will imperfectly than strive to serve Him lest he fail in the attempt.

DEALING DEATH TO DOUBT

Charles Haddon Spurgeon, the great British evangelist (1834–1892), recommended conquering doubt in this way:

Search the Scriptures for yourself, and follow no rule but that which is inspired. Take your light directly from the Sun. Let Holy Scripture be your unquestioned rule of faith and practice. If there is any point about which you are uncertain, I charge you by your loyalty to Christ, if you are His friend, to try to find out what His will is. Once you are sure on that point, never mind the human authorities or dignities who oppose His law. Let there be no question, no hesitation, no delay. If He commands you, carry out His will, though the gates of hell thunder at you.

from chapter 5, *Being God's Friend*

THE SILENCES OF GOD

George Macdonald (1824–1905), the Scottish novelist and poet, knew, as we do, both the great silences of God and the depths of His love:

He has an especial tenderness of love towards thee for that thou are in the dark and hast no light, and His heart is glad when thou dost arise and say, "I will go to my Father." For He sees thee through all the gloom through which thou canst not see Him. Say to Him, "My God, I am very dull and low and hard; but Thou are wise and high and tender; and Thou art my God. I am Thy child. Forsake me not." Then fold the arms of Thy faith and wait in quietness until light goes up in the darkness.

QUIETING OUR SOUL IN A BUSY WORLD

One of the most important—and difficult—"helps to hearing" is to quiet our busy souls and listen. Madame Guyon, the French mystic (1648–1717), suggests:

As you remain quiet, the presence of His Word in your spirit is in some degree a capacity for the reception of Himself. Perhaps it is during this time of silence that God may choose to speak to you. Hearing is a passive rather than active procedure. Rest. Rest. Rest in God's love. The only work you are required to do is to give your most intense attention to His still, small voice within. . . . Forget about yourself and all your household and occupational interests. Simply listen and be attentive to God. These passive actions will permit God to communicate His love to you. . . . You should repeat the process of becoming internally quiet as often as distractions occur. . . .

from "The Reward of Silence,"
Experiencing God through Prayer

BEING PATIENT IN THE SMALL THINGS

As we practice discernment in seemingly insignificant matters, we realize that as part of the process we learn to lay down our wills and our timing. Isaac Penington (1617–1680), a zealous Quaker, wrote:

Oh! look not after great things: small breathings, small desires after the Lord, if true and pure, are sweet beginnings of life. Take heed of despising "the day of small things," by looking after some great visitation, proportionable to thy distress, according to thy eye. Nay, thou must become a child; thou must lose thy own will quite by degrees. Thou must wait for life to be measured out by the Father and be content with what proportion, and at what time, He shall please to measure.

As you seek to grow in knowing and hearing God, be patient; He will enable you.

Glimpsing Our Goal

One of the goals of this book has been to help us to learn to take every thought captive to Christ. We have begun by letting Him renew our minds—perhaps, first, about our own selves. We have also taken tenuous steps in discernment as we ferret out which of three sources—self, Satan or the Holy Spirit—gives rise to each of our thoughts or emotions.

We looked at tests we can use to make sure the source of an idea is the only one that tells us the whole truth: Jesus' Holy Spirit living in us. We caught a glimmer of God's endless grace

201

in forgiving us when we stumble over a hurdle or fail in discernment. We jogged through the fun side of discernment—the nudges and knowings He sometimes gives. And we power-walked through the places where we will not hear the Lord's voice: the doubts, fears, worries and vague guilts that hamstring us, trying to trip us up and keep us from finishing our race. We found encouraging suggestions to get us past the hindrances we face along the way as we run our course. And finally we noted that just as Jesus, our Coach, always heard from His Father, we too, can listen to the voice in our helmets. Those He has coached before us cheer us on, unseen, from heavenly grandstands.

For a season you and I have run alongside each other, as we keep pace toward the goals the Lord has set up in our lives.

Where am I in learning to take every thought captive to Christ? In a nutshell, miles down the road from where I was 25 years ago! But I have miles yet to go. In some areas I am more consistent than in others. Often now I stop a thought process cold and ask, "Is that You, Lord?" or I turn it into prayer. I recognize nudges to intercede for someone or something, and do this many times a day, most days. I am fairly adept at knowing what is *not* the Lord's voice. I can run many of the primary and pocket tests in chapters 5 and 6 quickly. This means that most of the time I can spot the unholy spirit and rebuke or ignore the ideas he has planted.

I am not as quick at knowing my Shepherd's voice, but I am listening more all the time. I still (and always will) have to watch my "self" carefully. I am good at rebelling and having to go to the ocean of grace for more forgiveness.

Just last week I received an e-mail from a friend that enraged me. I fired off an answer at once, choosing not to ask the Lord what He wanted me to say. I knew the attitude He wanted: love and forgiveness and gentleness. But I wanted to blow off steam.

Within a few minutes the Lord convicted me, and I sent off a second e-mail saying, "I was miffed and squiffed. And I deliberately did not ask the Lord. Please, forgive?"

She wrote back, "Of course! What's miffed and squiffed between old friends?"

The biggest changes for me have come as I no longer entertain fear-filled and anxiety-ridden thoughts. Even better, because I have rejected them so many times and turned toward the Lord, I am enjoying an ever-strengthening trust in Him that is fast outpacing any fear.

I no longer rely on feeling God's love or presence to verify His reality in my life. I accept, and then know, that He is always here. Sometimes the feelings are here, too. I still like that best!

Turning my thoughts to the Lord over and over has made me sense His closeness more. As I increasingly glimpse His love and power, I am able to let go and just let Him be. I can lean back on His will, not just trusting that it is best but *knowing* that it is. Religion has become a relationship.

So I continue in my race, rejoicing at the ever-increasing strength in my faith muscles.

You, too, are growing in spiritual strength and endurance. Remember these basics: Your Father loves you dearly. He longs for communion and communication with you. He has given you Scripture so you can hear Him. He has revealed the ultimate possibilities of discernment in Jesus Christ, His Son. And He has shown, in the believers who have gone ahead, that a life lived closer and closer to His great heart can be a reality for you, too. Deeper levels of discernment will change you forever and fit you for the best part of life—the one yet to come. Practicing discernment will move you beyond what the Lord wants and take you to who He is. It will take you to Him.

My prayers for your growth in hearing God's voice for your life come with this book. They are beautifully expressed in a prayer attributed to Benedict of Nursia (480–543):

Gracious and holy Father, please give me
intellect to understand You, reason to discern You,
diligence to seek You, wisdom to find You,

a spirit to know You, a heart to meditate upon You,
ears to hear You, eyes to see You, a tongue to proclaim You,
patience to wait for You, and perseverance to look for You.
Grant me a perfect end—Your holy presence,
    a blessed resurrection,
and life everlasting.

Amen!

Your Turn to Discern

Many books that share ideas about how to perform a particular task or learn to do something end with a section encouraging you to begin to put it into practice. From the very first chapter of this book, however, I asked—and prayed—that you would start practicing discernment.

1. How is it coming for you? How is it easier to know the Lord's voice? Where is it still difficult?

2. In what areas do you see the Lord wanting to change you? (Not the areas *you* want to see changed, but the ones where you believe He desires to work.)

3. Do you see yourself differently than you did on the first page of this book? How?

4. Do you see the Lord differently than you did on page 1? In what ways?

Note: If you would like to share your thoughts and progress with me, I would love to hear from you. You may write me care of my publisher or e-mail me at <isthatyoulord@mail.com>. May you go for the gold!

Postscript

Conversations with *What* God?

In the Prologue I referred to a book and an interview as the catalysts precipitating my writing about spiritual discernment. Here are a few samples—first from the book *Conversations with God* by Neale Donald Walsch (Putnam, 1995), then from my interview with a person who underwent an out-of-body experience.

After reading these excerpts, you will easily discern why my heart longed to write *Is That You, Lord?*

The Book

On page 8 of the book *Conversations with God,* the being the author calls *God* tells him, "I cannot tell you my truth until you stop telling me yours."

"But my truth comes from you."

"Who said so?"

"Others."

"What others?"

"Leaders. Ministers. Rabbis. Priests. Books. The *Bible,* for heaven's sake!"

[God replies,] "Those are not authoritative sources."

Two paragraphs later God continues, "Listen to your feelings. Listen to your Highest Thoughts. Listen to your experience. Whenever any one of these differs from what you've been told by your teachers or read in your books, forget the words. *Words are the least reliable purveyor of Truth.*"

(These italics, incidentally, are the author's.)

As this god reveals himself, it is clear that he is not the One Christians follow. He would like us to believe that whatever we want to think or feel is true. Most especially he wants us to doubt any link between *words* and *truth*—a link the New Testament makes repeatedly. Here are just three examples from the gospel of John: "In the beginning was the Word, and the Word was with God, and the Word was God. . . . The Word became flesh and made his dwelling among us" (John 1:1, 14). "Jesus answered, 'I am . . . the truth. . . . No one comes to the Father except through Me'" (John 14:6).

The god of these conversations, on the other hand, would have us doubt and discard Jesus, the living Word and the very embodiment of Truth.

On page 197 of *Conversations with God* comes this interchange between "God" and the writer. "God" speaks first. The emphases, once again, are the author's.

> "YOU ARE MY BODY. Just as your body is to your mind and soul, so, too, are *you* to *my* mind and soul. *Everything I experience, I experience through you.* . . . So it is that Jesus of Nazareth, among the many who understood this mystery, spoke immutable truth when he said, '*I and the Father are One.*' Now I will tell you there are even larger truths than this to which you will one day become privy, for even as you are the body of me, I am the body of another."
>
> "You mean you are *not* God?"
>
> "Yes, I am God, as you now understand Him. I am Goddess as you now comprehend Her. I am the Conceiver and the Creator of Everything you now know and experience, and you are my children . . . even as I am the child of another."

By now I am sure you have figured out who this god's father is. Listen to Jesus: "You belong to your father, the devil, and you want to carry out your father's desire. He was a murderer from the beginning, not holding to the truth, for there is no truth in him. When he lies, he speaks his native language, for he is a liar and the father of lies" (John 8:44).

It is inevitable for a believer to conclude, then, that the author of this book has had an encounter with a counterfeit angel of light: "Such men are false apostles, deceitful workmen, masquerading as apostles of Christ. And no wonder, for Satan himself masquerades as an angel of light. It is not surprising, then, if his servants masquerade as servants of righteousness" (2 Corinthians 11:13–15).

Although Neale Donald Walsch does not claim to be a Christian, he does capitalize *God* on the flyleaf and throughout the book. His publisher is implying that he is hearing and passing on information from the Judeo-Christian God. Nor does he offer any other name for this "god." But the god of these conversations shares ideas diametrically opposed to what we read in the Bible and hear from Jesus. This gives us a clear choice. Who is the God of these conversations? Both Scripture and this book of "conversations with God" cannot be true. Only one is true. We must choose which.

The Interview

In my interview, Jessie, as I will call this person, related that while doctors on the outside were struggling to save his life, he found himself moving out of his body toward "a cross of light." From that light a being emerged, arms stretched forward in welcome. The light being, whom Jessie assumed was Jesus, embraced him, then said he would have to go back. First, though, this God invited him to sit and talk and relax.

207

They sat on a bench by a small stream with a bridge across it. The grass was a vibrant, shimmering green around them. God invited Jessie to ask him anything.

"What hurts you that we do the most?" Jessie asked.

"That people don't love each other because they are born different colors or with disabilities. I love man, but it hurts me to see them kill my other children."

What about salvation and eternal life?

"We are flexible," he responded. "We make it up as we go along." And he implied that there was nothing to fear, because everyone was saved.

"What about someone like Hitler?"

The being laughed. "Well, we send him back until he gets it right, but of course there is a limit to that."

Later in their conversation, before the doctors stabilized Jessie and he found himself back in the hospital room, this God told him there were really four parts to the Trinity.

"The fourth part is angels," he explained.

What about this encounter from a biblical standpoint? How about the content of what this being told Jessie?

As much as this being may have looked and seemed like Jesus, he was not. Again, he had to be Satan masquerading as an angel of light. How do we know this? Let's look at some of the answers to the questions in light of Scripture and what Jesus said.

What hurts God the most, according to His Word?

"You do not believe the one [God] sent," declared Jesus (John 5:38), after saying clearly that God the Father had sent Him.

What about everyone being saved? Peter declared boldly to the religious leaders in Jerusalem about Jesus Christ of Nazareth, "Salvation is found in no one else, for there is no other name under heaven given to men by which we must be saved" (Acts 4:12). Our God has made provision for every human being to be saved. But, sadly, not all choose that salvation. "If you do not believe that I am the one I claim to be,"

Jesus told the Jews, "you will indeed die in your sins" (John 8:24).

What about Hitler being reincarnated? The idea of reincarnation runs counter to Scripture: "Man is destined to die once, and after that to face judgment" (Hebrews 9:27).

Before I knew the Lord, I toyed around with believing in reincarnation. But I found that it made no sense. No one has any way to know what he or she did in any previous incarnation; and the goal of all these good works, in any case, is nirvana, or a kind of nothingness. How glad I am to know that I will ultimately shed this body for an eternally alive, resurrected one in the presence of Absolute Love!

How about angels being co-equal with the triune Godhead?

Our old enemy would love for us to believe this; it was his original sin-wish (see Isaiah 14:13–14)! The Godhead described in the New Testament, however, has only three Persons: Father, Son and Holy Spirit (see Matthew 28:19). And the worship of angels is forbidden (see Colossians 2:18).

The "God" with whom Jessie spoke set up standards in opposition to Scripture. Once again, it is our choice whom to believe.

No matter when or how some spirit reveals itself to us (looking like Jesus or an angel or an extraterrestrial!), no matter how strongly we think it is Jesus, we must obey 1 John 4:1–3:

> Dear friends, do not believe every spirit, but test the spirits to see whether they are from God, because many false prophets have gone out into the world. This is how you can recognize the Spirit of God: Every spirit that acknowledges that Jesus Christ has come in the flesh is from God, but every spirit that does not acknowledge Jesus is not from God.

Any being claiming to be an angel of light will respond to the question "By the way, can you confess that Jesus Christ has come in the flesh?" If such a being is not from God, there will most likely be a giant *Pouf!* and the event will end in a cloud of smoke. If it is a true angel, he will remain, and if it is Jesus whom we are questioning, through the Holy Spirit, He will not be offended in the least. He is the One who told us to do this, and He will be delighted that we are testing obediently to be sure it is He with whom we speak.

There *are* angels of light—created beings who stay true to God, "the Father of the heavenly lights" (James 1:17). Even we ourselves "were once darkness, but now [we] are light in the Lord" (Ephesians 5:8).

On the dedication page of this book, I quoted lyrics from Lisa Adams' song "Father of Light." I pray that in the pages since, you have seen Him shine through and have caught a brighter glimpse of His love. Thank you for taking this journey with me.

Books for the Journey

A Few of the Books That Have Contained God's Voice for Me

Arthur, Kay. *How to Study Your Bible*. Eugene, Ore.: Harvest House, 1994.

Barber, Karen. *Ready, Set, Wait: Help for Life on Hold*. Grand Rapids, Mich.: Baker, 1996.

Basham, Don. *Deliver Us from Evil*. Grand Rapids, Mich.: Chosen, 1972.

Blair, Charles, with Judy Stonecipher. *Lose the Weight of the World: The Five-Day Spiritual Fitness Plan for Your Soul*. Green Forest, Ark.: New Leaf, 1997.

Brother Lawrence. *The Practice of the Presence of God*. Pittsburgh: Whitaker, 1982.

Carothers, Merlin R. *From Fear to Faith*. Nashville: Thomas Nelson, 1997.

———. *Power in Praise*. Escondido, Calif.: Merlin R. Carothers, 1972.

———. *Prison to Praise*. Escondido, Calif.: Merlin R. Carothers, 1970.

Christenson, Evelyn. *Lord, Change Me!* Wheaton, Ill.: Victor, 1977.

————. *What Happens When Women Pray*. Wheaton, Ill.: Victor, 1975.

Christenson, Larry. *The Christian Family*. Minneapolis: Bethany, 1970.

————. *The Renewed Mind*. Minneapolis: Bethany, 1974.

Foster, Richard. *Prayer: Finding the Heart's True Home*. San Francisco: HarperSanFrancisco, 1992.

Freeman, Joel. *God Is Not Fair: Coming to Terms with Life's Raw Deals*. San Bernardino, Calif.: Here's Life, 1987.

Graham, Billy. *Angels: God's Secret Agents*. New York: Doubleday, 1975.

————. *Just as I Am*. New York: HarperCollins, 1997.

Hazard, David. *Safe within Your Love: A Forty-Day Journey in the Company of Hannah W. Smith*. Minneapolis: Bethany, 1992.

Keller, Phillip. *A Shepherd Looks at Psalm 23*. Grand Rapids, Mich.: Zondervan, 1970.

Lucado, Max. *In the Grip of Grace*. Dallas: Word, 1996.

Manning, Brennan. *Abba's Child: The Cry of the Heart for Intimate Belonging*. Colorado Springs: NavPress, 1994.

Marshall, Catherine. *Beyond Our Selves*. New York: Avon, 1961.

————. *A Closer Walk*. Old Tappan, N.J.: Chosen, 1986.

————. *The Helper*. Waco, Tex.: Chosen, 1978.

————. *Meeting God at Every Turn*. Lincoln, Va.: Chosen, 1980.

————. *Something More*. New York: McGraw-Hill, 1974.

McDowell, Josh. *Evidence that Demands a Verdict: Historical Evidence for the Christian Faith*. San Bernardino, Calif.: Campus Crusade, 1972.

McGee, Robert S. *The Search for Significance*. Houston: Rapha, 1990.

Peale, Mrs. Norman Vincent (Ruth). *The Adventure of Being a Wife*. Greenwich, Conn.: Fawcett, 1971.

Peretti, Frank E. *This Present Darkness*. Westchester, Ill.: Crossway, 1986.

Philips, J. B. *Your God Is Too Small*. New York: Macmillan, 1972.

Prince, Derek. *Shaping History through Prayer and Fasting*. New Kensington, Pa.: Whitaker, 1973.

————. *Spiritual Warfare*. New Kensington, Pa.: Whitaker, 1987.

Rinker, Rosalind. *Communicating Love through Prayer*. Grand Rapids, Mich.: Zondervan, 1966.

————. *Prayer: Conversing with God*. Grand Rapids, Mich.: Zondervan, 1959.

Sheldon, Charles M. *In His Steps*. New Kensington, Pa.: Whitaker, 1979 (orig. 1897).

Smith, Hannah Whitall. *The Christian's Secret of a Happy Life*. Old Tappan, N.J.: Revell, 1970.

————. *The God of All Comfort*. Chicago: Moody, 1956.

Swindoll, Charles R. *Improving Your Serve: The Art of Unselfish Living*. Waco, Tex.: Word, 1981.

Tileson, Mary. *Daily Strength for Daily Needs*. New Kensington, Pa.: Whitaker, 1997.

Tirabassi, Becky. *Let Prayer Change Your Life*. Nashville: Thomas Nelson, 1990.

Tryon, Howard Jr. *Praying for You*. Grand Rapids, Mich.: Kregel, 1996.

Wardle, Terry. *Whispers of Love in Seasons of Fear*. Grand Rapids, Mich.: Chosen, 1999.

Yancey, Philip. *The Jesus I Never Knew*. Grand Rapids, Mich.: Zondervan, 1995.

————. *What's So Amazing about Grace?* Grand Rapids, Mich.: Zondervan, 1997.

Roberta Rogers has published in *Guideposts, Daily Guideposts, Guideposts for Teens* and various periodicals, and has experience as an administrator, a Bible study creator and presenter, and the director of communications for her church. She has also designed and taught writing courses for home-schooled students.

She and her husband, Bill, are finishing their fourth decade of marriage. They have four grown, uniquely individual sons. Although scattered to far-flung places, they remain a close family—something that delights Roberta (or Bobbi, as her friends call her) most of all. Bill and Bobbi currently live in Maryland.